No one rider has left such an indelible mark on New Zealand cycling as the fabulous O'Shea, who reigned supreme on the road from 1911 to 1924.

The Otago Daily Times, 28 September 1962

New Zealand Cycling Legends 01

Phil O'Shea
WIZARD ON WHEELS

Jonathan Kennett & Bronwen Wall

Copyright © 2005 The Kennett Brothers

Published by The Kennett Brothers
in association with Whitireia Publishing

PO Box 11 310, Wellington, New Zealand
Phone/fax +64 4 499 6376

jonathan@kennett.co.nz
www.kennett.co.nz

ISBN 0-95834-908-8

Every effort has been made to ensure that the information in this
book is accurate. The authors/publishers will be glad to rectify any
omissions at the earliest opportunity.

Front cover photograph: Phil O'Shea, immediately after winning the
1911 Christchurch to Timaru Road Race. Canterbury Museum, The
Lyttelton Times Collection, 1805 1/2 (detail).

Back cover photograph: A life-size print of this portrait of O'Shea
on his Jones track racing bike hung above the counter of Jones Cycles
during the 1920s and 30s. O'Shea Collection.

Editing, typesetting and production by Jackie Bedford, Anna Craig,
Celestina Sumby and Penelope Whitson, Whitireia Diploma in
Publishing

Design by Anna Brown

Printed and bound in New Zealand by Astra Print

CONTENTS

PROLOGUE

This biography was born from *RIDE: The story of cycling in New Zealand*. While writing *RIDE,* we often lamented the fact that the stories of outstanding champions had to be condensed to fit in a single page or less. "Not enough," we thought. Their lives are fascinating because they succeeded in attaining the aspirations that most of us share. On their hard path to sporting stardom they all suffered pain and defeat, as well as euphoria and victory. Their inspiring feats deserved more – much more. And so the series *New Zealand Cycling Legends* took form.

Why start with Phil O'Shea? He's a comparative unknown alongside the likes of Tino Tabak, Warwick Dalton and Sarah Ulmer. The most compelling reason was time. O'Shea is the earliest of the ten legends to be portrayed in this series and the element of time has eroded his story more than the others. Inevitably, records and photos relating to his career have been lost, and most of those who witnessed him race have passed away. The pieces of O'Shea's past that remain are scattered around the country. Some are safe in libraries and museums; many more are stored in faded shoeboxes and rusty Griffins biscuit tins. This gave the writing a sense of urgency. Throughout the six months of research the message from eyewitnesses and newspapers has been compelling and consistent – O'Shea was the greatest all-round cyclist New Zealand has ever produced.

This is the first extensive account of Phil O'Shea's life and racing career. It is set against the backdrop of a golden era for cycling. O'Shea was born in the cycling city of Christchurch in 1889. The modern safety bicycle had just been invented – overtaking the elegant penny farthing and sparking a worldwide bicycle boom. As a result, cycle racing in New Zealand in the early 1900s was a major sport. Vast crowds thronged to watch with fascination the displays of daring, spills, good sportsmanship, sheer strength and determination of famous wheelmen.

The exploits and outstanding performances of the early New Zealand racing cyclists have not always been fully appreciated. Research is beginning to show that their achievements have been underrated, especially considering the equipment they used and the roads they raced on.

In O'Shea's day, road riders had to endure tough and uncompromising conditions, riding on heavy fixed-wheel bikes, often with no brakes. Dirt and shingle roads, sometimes repaired with chunky rocks, caused frequent punctures. Streams and rivers had to be forded. DNFs (Did Not Finish) were common, but the first mud-covered riders to reach the finish were guaranteed a hero's welcome. And the actual results? Incredible! In 1913, O'Shea covered the 180 dusty and rocky kilometres between Timaru and Christchurch in 5 hours 14 minutes 58 seconds.

Despite riding much of it alone, on a relatively heavy bicycle, he averaged 34.3 kilometres per hour.

O'Shea endured the tough conditions better than anybody, crossing finish lines with bent handlebars, flat tyres, buckled wheels, gashes to the head and even a dislocated shoulder. When required, he had an unbeatable sprint at the end of the longest races, honed by his brilliance on the track.

The hallmarks of O'Shea's career were the amazing speed with which he rose to the top and the length of time he stayed there. Within two years of entering his first race in 1909 he had become road champion of New Zealand – and Australasia.

After successes in the 1913 national track championships and record-breaking wins in both the Timaru to Christchurch and the Taranaki Round-the-Mountain classics, one newspaper commented, "O'Shea has for some years now proved himself absolutely invincible on the roads, and is without doubt the best rider in Australasia."[1] A decade later, nothing had changed. He was still the Australasian Road Champion.

O'Shea remained at the top for 20 years, winning his last New Zealand track titles in 1930, aged 41. Despite his modesty, he was a sporting superstar, attracting thousands of spectators each time he matched his skills against world-class challengers.

Phil O'Shea was a champion of champions. His victories – from ¼-mile sprints to 265-kilometre road races – earned him the moniker "wizard on wheels".

RISE OF A CHAMPION

A gale of laughter flew down the narrow train carriage. It was Friday 29 October 1909, and the Southern Express was making its daily trip south across the Canterbury Plains. Passengers, lulled by the train's monotonous rocking and the vast, empty landscape, stirred and looked across to the huddle of young men who had raised such a guffaw. The group was heading to Timaru, to compete in the next day's Great Timaru to Christchurch Road Race.

Spirits were high as the men chatted and compared training strategies, but for the moment, attention centred on two of the party. One was a famous cycling champion, tall and bursting with energy and strength: everyone knew Jack Arnst. The other was a young stranger by the name of Phil O'Shea. Short, dark and reticent, O'Shea had three things in his favour: a fierce determination, an innate grasp of tactics and a hidden confidence that belied his small stature.

Earlier, O'Shea had sidled up to the group, eager to soak up the camaraderie. Catching his eye, Arnst sized up the bow-legged bantam and asked, "Where are you going, sonny?"

"I'm racing the Timaru to Christchurch," replied O'Shea.

"The Timaru to Christchurch?" Arnst repeated. "You've got to be joking! You won't make it half way." The accompanying laughter came from men who had ridden the arduous race before. It kindled in O'Shea the fire of his Irish-roots stubbornness. "I'll bloody show you," he thought.[1]

The following day, Arnst told a reporter from the Chrischurch paper *The Press* it had been the hardest race he had ever ridden. And O'Shea? After battling it out over 112 miles of unsealed roads, mostly into a headwind, he was part of the lead bunch that slogged its way into the Plumpton Racecourse in Christchurch. Into the final straight, O'Shea suddenly shot ahead, leaving the rest struggling to catch his wheel, but the gap simply got larger. He won by 20 yards and "was

O'Shea is carried from the finish line of the 1923 Timaru to Christchurch Road Race.

Weekly News

carried off shoulder-high" with excited spectators "cheering him to the echo".[2]

Over the next two years, O'Shea was to become the road cycling champion of Canterbury, the South Island, New Zealand and then Australasia. An incredible feat from such unlikely beginnings.

Phil O'Shea struggled into this world on 16 April 1889. His twin died at birth. Throughout childhood O'Shea doggedly battled recurring bouts of quinsy (a serious infection that develops into painful abscesses around the tonsils). O'Shea's throat would swell up, his temperature would skyrocket and his jaw muscles spasm. At such times, it was often difficult for him to eat or even speak. Little wonder he grew into a weedy, round-shouldered lightweight. Despite his father being a solid, towering presence over 6 feet tall, Phil barely reached 5 foot 6 inches and weighed in at a slight 8 stone 7 pounds (54 kilograms). "Up to about nineteen years of age I was subject to illness. I was a weakling. But when I took up cycling I developed. It seemed to suit me."[3] (Within two years of rigorous cycling, his weight had increased to 11 stone 2 pounds.) What he initially lacked in size, O'Shea made up for with sheer determination and a cunning game plan.

O'Shea's throat would swell up, his temperature would skyrocket and his jaw muscles spasm.

THE DARK HORSE

He had the element of surprise, and he knew it. As a virtual unknown to the cycling arena, Phil O'Shea was welcomed into the sport with a generous handicap for the 1909 Timaru to Christchurch Road

In 1903, Jack Arnst
won fastest time
in the Timaru to
Christchurch and won
the Warrnambool to
Melbourne, setting a new
record in the process.
Years later, O'Shea said,
"Jack Arnst was the most
wonderful rider of my
time. ... Even when I was
climbing up and trying to
oust him from first, he
would often shout a word
of encouragement in
a race."[4]

Race, starting 45 minutes before the scratch riders, including his hero Jack Arnst.

O'Shea's rivals hardly expected the scrawny new-comer to finish, let alone lead the front bunch into Christchurch and convincingly out-sprint them in the home straight. But O'Shea had been following the tactics of cycling for years through the news-papers – his carefully indexed scrapbook of articles and newspaper reports, dating back to 1897, bears the proof. He knew exactly what he was doing: his chances of winning were never going to be so good again. On 24 October, one week before the Timaru to Christchurch, O'Shea slipped into gear by entering his first track race. His goals for the minor event in Chertsey, a small town just north of Ashburton, were to win race tyres and prepare himself for his dream challenge the next weekend; he achieved both.

O'Shea had trained quietly but determinedly for the great race. As one news reporter wrote after the win: "When the opportunity served he took a hundred-mile spin during his week-ends, but beyond that he made no extra preparation for his task."[5] Such training rides followed a week of hard physical work as a packer in the warehouse of Messrs Henry Berry and Company, followed by a day of cricket in summer, or in winter, a good tough game of rugby. A "hundred-mile spin" to round off the weekend could hardly translate to a stroll in the park, and yet this is the impression O'Shea gave.

Until 1909, O'Shea had been known as a promising cricket and rugby player. One official later stated:

"As sure as I am sitting here, he would have been a Canterbury, even a New Zealand representative, had he kept on with cricket."[6] O'Shea told almost no one of his growing passion for cycling, and it was with considerable surprise that a member of his cricket team learned of O'Shea's entry in the Timaru to Christchurch race. "In the middle of one week he told us he would not be available for the next match. He said nothing about a big cycling event coming up. It was much to our surprise that we read in next Saturday night's paper that a youth of 20 named Phil O'Shea had won the Timaru to Christchurch."[7]

A SURE BET

Though not a gambling man, O'Shea was so sure of his cycling ability that he asked his brother Bob to place a bet on him to win the Timaru to Christchurch that first year. As O'Shea was a rank outsider, the winnings for such a bet would have amounted to a small fortune. Unfortunately, his brother's faith did not match Phil's own. Bob anxiously followed race progress over the radio, but no word came through on Phil. As the race passed through Ashburton and still no mention was made of O'Shea, Bob decided not to place the bet. Who could blame him? A brisk nor'easter had increased to gale strength; the roads were "liberally strewn with gorse, which had blown from adjacent hedges"[8] causing worn tyres to puncture; beyond the Rangitata River crossing, the notorious Maronan road section lay thick with shingle; not to mention the numerous pools of water

"To me, the race never started until Ashburton. I used to try and get there as fresh as when I set off. Then I'd really tear into it."[11]

and stream crossings. Crashes and mechanical mishaps triggered by the torturous course "made the race a very trying one"[9] and "those who were not well-seasoned had to throw up the sponge before they had covered half the distance".[10]

By two o'clock, roughly 2,000 spectators jostled for space at the Plumpton Racecourse to witness the finish. *The Press* reported: "There were five dust-grimed, straining toilers in the [first] bunch ..." with O'Shea at the front. "Each was flying signals of distress. ... Fighting against the full force of the head wind, [they] crawled along with painful slowness. Rounding the eastern corner, still wheel to wheel, the competitors began to draw upon their little remaining reserves of strength, and ... coming into the straight they all sprinted magnificently. O'Shea jumped away ..." and won by 20 yards in a time of 7 hours 6 minutes 55 seconds.

O'Shea had not come through unscathed however. Newspaper reports had him in the lead when he stopped for a mug of milk at the Rangitata feeding station. Following close behind, another competitor came in for refreshments too fast and ran into O'Shea's bike, buckling one of the wheels (in 1909 none of the racing bikes had brakes). "This damage could not be repaired properly so the plucky young rider continued the race on an untrue wheel ...."[12] Other reports suggest O'Shea had a second spill "on this side of Ashburton, which shook him a good deal but did no serious damage".[13] With determination that was to become a hallmark, O'Shea plugged on.

Why was O'Shea never referred to on the radio updates his brother was listening to? Perhaps as an unknown rider he was considered too insignificant to warrant a mention, perhaps he didn't hand across the identifying paper tickets to marshals in towns as he passed through, or perhaps the tickets were blown away in the strong wind. Whatever the case, Phil did not speak to his brother for two years for failing to place the bet. No doubt, the £40 winner's prize (the equivalent of four months' wages) was of some consolation.

THE REALITY OF RACING

O'Shea's initial success encouraged him to take up cycling seriously, but the following year was hard – especially as the advantage of being an unknown was gone. He competed regularly in Canterbury road and track races, but in the 1910 Timaru to Christchurch event he was given only an 8-minute head start over the scratch bunch and did not get a top placing. He even tried his luck in Australia, again with no great success, although his results (third fastest time in the 204-kilometre Goulburn to Sydney Road Race and fifth fastest time in the 265-kilometre Warrnambool to Melbourne Road Race) certainly showed potential.

O'Shea returned to New Zealand and trained with more determination than ever. The results were phenomenal.

Rather than being put off by such failure, O'Shea returned to New Zealand and trained with more determination than ever. The results were phenomenal.

In 1911, O'Shea was virtually unbeatable on the

A foggy start to the 1911 Christchurch to Timaru Road Race.

The Weekly Press

road. Newspaper articles indicate that, barring a few occasions when he had mechanical problems, the "wizard on wheels"[14] won every race he entered.

The 1911 Christchurch to Timaru (raced in reverse to allow the Timaru public to see the finish) was the country's biggest road race that year, earning the fastest rider the title of Road Champion of New Zealand and the opportunity to represent New Zealand in the Australasian Road Racing Championship. This time, O'Shea started at the back with the scratch riders. He rode with them to Temuka, then disaster struck: "… a dog got in O'Shea's way. In dodging the animal, O'Shea came a nasty cropper, falling on to the top of his head. … He was dazed, and his head was bleeding severely, and there were several bad cuts and bruises on his body."[15]

Despite his injuries, O'Shea quickly remounted,

and although the bleeding continued for the remaining 20 kilometres to Timaru, he finished with the fastest time of 5 hours 37 minutes, securing the championship title and a place on the New Zealand team. After the race, he received eight stitches and was found by a *Lyttelton Times* reporter with "his head swathed in bandages".[16] Even at this early stage of his career, O'Shea was winning mass spectator support and the respect of his fellow riders – "He is held in high esteem by his fellow competitors, who were pleased at his success …" He was also earning himself a reputation as "a gentleman at every stage of the game".[17]

For O'Shea, the real test was to follow in the Warrnambool to Melbourne, which doubled that year as the Australasian Road Racing Championship. The course of 165 miles (265 kilometres) was a gruelling grind over shingle and dirt roads. "I never felt sanguine of my chance of being first, but I was out for the blue ribbon and meant to take it to New

Phil O'Shea leads through a waterway during the 1911 Christchurch to Timaru Road Race.

The Weekly Press

HANDICAP KILLERS

Racers of O'Shea's time competed in both handicap and scratch races. Almost all road races and about half of the track races were handicapped. Handicaps were, and still are, calculated from previous race performances. An official estimates how long each entrant is likely to take to complete an event, then allocates different start times, sending the slowest riders off first and the fastest last. The aim is to give everyone an equal chance of winning. This egalitarian system may be complicated for the riders, but it encourages participation and provides great interest for the spectators. The finishes are often close and the outcome always uncertain.

Handicap racing is still common in New Zealand in local club-organised events. Beyond Australasia, where competitor numbers are higher, handicap racing is uncommon.

As an established rider, O'Shea invariably started in the 'scratch bunch', which in a long road race (e.g. 180 kilometres) left up to 55 minutes after the first riders. Winning a handicap race from scratch was hard work – especially if he was the only one in the scratch bunch!

"Racing alone from the back mark against riders who had fantastic handicaps was too punishing," O'Shea recalled later. "It killed competition as well as the rider ... the most stout-hearted cyclist was discouraged to know he would only meet the front markers on his last lap."[18]

The scratch men rarely won 'line honours', but there was also the lure of winning 'fastest time' honours – which O'Shea usually rode away with. In road championship races, the first across the line won the race but the fastest rider became the 'champion'.

Track racing featured handicap races as well as 'scratch races' (where all riders start together). All track championship events and match races were scratch races. In his first season of track racing at English Park Stadium, O'Shea appeared in two meetings a week and lost only one scratch race.

A New Zealand representative portrait of Phil O'Shea.

Zealand if hard riding could do it," O'Shea later said. With 340 competitors (10 of them Kiwis) and 100,000 spectators, this was the Australasian sporting spectacle of the year.

Twenty-thousand people thronged the last half-mile to the finish at Haymarket in Melbourne. With excitement running high, marshals found it difficult to keep people off the course. In fact, once the first six competitors had finished, the crowd could no longer be held at bay, surging over barriers, swarming through the finish area and making progress difficult for the following riders. Apart from when he crashed into one of the spectators near the finish, O'Shea sat in the saddle for the 8 hours 18 minutes it took him to battle the wind and strong competition from Australian Albert Pianta, winning fastest time and

The two-man-team format for six-day races was introduced after American legislation forbade any contestant from racing for more than 12 hours a day.

the Australasian Road Racing Championship.

Considering O'Shea had started racing just two years earlier, this was a meteoric rise to sporting stardom. The fact was not lost on appreciative fans. Along with Jack Arnst, O'Shea earned himself the title "Ace of the Road", and enthusiasts eagerly anticipated his future races. O'Shea was not to disappoint them, but cycling is a sport of infinite variables – victory is never assured.

A LOW YEAR

The next year was a forgettable racing year for O'Shea. Despite doing well in local track and road races, the big wins eluded him. He tore a tyre in that year's Timaru to Christchurch and finished 36th overall. At the end of the year, he crossed 'the ditch' with A.B.L. 'Smiler' Smith to compete in a six-day track race at the Sydney Oval.

A jam occurs when one rider tries to make a break and lap the field, gaining a valuable lead, extra points and special bonus money. In the Sydney Six-day Cycle Marathon, there were no successful jams.

Back then, six days meant six days. Competition was fierce as teams battled it out non-stop, rain or shine, for 141 hours. Either O'Shea or Smiler had to be racing at all times. On the fourth day, after covering 2,344 kilometres, the Kiwi pair lay in second place. The weather was bad that day, often forcing riders to stop and swap their lightweight track machines for heavy, wide-tyred road bikes. "There was a terrific downpour at 3:45 pm and the riders were all drenched to the skin. They changed on to roadster machines and took to the asphalt again with overcoats on. This meant very slow work until the track dried."[19]

By the sixth day Smiler was feeling unwell, and it

was left to O'Shea to pull up the slack. He did so with characteristic grit and determination "… ever to be seen well up among the field in the fiercest jams".[20] Some 25,000 spectators crammed around the Sydney Oval to witness the finish.

First place went to an experienced six-day racer, Australian Reginald 'Iron Man' McNamara. McNamara had made a specialty of 'sixers', racing over 150 around the world during his 22-year career and winning an estimated US $500,000. He had also snapped his collarbone 16 times and broken both legs, one arm and numerous ribs.

Only 15 yards behind McNamara, in sixth place, completing his first (and last) six-day race was New Zealander Phil O'Shea. The first seven teams had all covered 2,949 kilometres – an average of 491 kilometres per day.

141 HOURS AWHEEL.

THE SIX DAYS' CYCLE RACE.

STARTED AT ONE O'CLOCK THIS MORNING.

BIG INTERNATIONAL CONTEST.

At 1 o'clock this morning the second annual six days' cycle race commenced at the Sydney Cricket Ground.

The riders who are contesting it will be on the track day and night, until next Saturday, at 10 p.m. The race is of 141 hours' duration, and open to teams of two riders, no rider to be on the track for more than 12 consecutive hours, or a total of 16 hours in any one day. Riders may relieve each other as often as they please.

Starting, as it did, in the small hours of the morning, there was an attendance of about 3000 when President A. E. O'Brien, of the League of Wheelmen, despatched the teams. Wet or fine, hail or shine, the riders will continue the race, and, if, at the finishing hour on Saturday, no team is one lap, or more, ahead of the others, then all teams that are equal will race three laps, and the order in which they finish will decide the destination of the prize-money.

Last year the prize for the race—which was won by Goullett and Hehir—was £1000. This year the riders divide 33 1-3 per cent. of the gross takings at the gates—an innovation in Australia.

PEAK PERFORMANCE

O'Shea's team may not have placed in the top three in the Sydney marathon, but the experience undoubtedly honed O'Shea's track racing skills. On his return to New Zealand, he achieved many great track successes. In March 1913, at the St. Patrick's Sports Day held at Lancaster Park, O'Shea won the ½-mile, 1-mile and 3-mile track races from the scratch mark (see photo on page 25). The following month, at the Easter sports in Temuka, he added the 1-mile and 2-mile scratch races to his tally. O'Shea

PHIL O'SHEA
SEE WHAT THE
SPEEDY has helped Phil
O'Shea to do.

1st in the 17½ Mile Kaiapoi Road
  Race from scratch.
1st in the 8 Mile Marshland Road
  Race from scratch.
1st in the 2 Mile £20 Wheel Race,
  St. Patrick's Sports, Grey-
  mouth.
1st in the 3 Mile Handicap Race,
  St. Patrick's Sports, Grey-
  mouth.

  Besides this Speedy riders have
secured 1st, and 3rd in galore.
If you want to win ride the cycle
that is easy to push.
  Note.—Phil O'Shea has won
more money, and put up more
records than any other rider in
New Zealand or Australia.

Jack Suckling
Sole Maker of SPEEDY Cycles
114 Manchester Street, Ch.Ch.

Jack Suckling's advertisement makes sure everyone knows what bike the young gun is riding.

O'Shea Collection

would soon combine this new-found speed with his proven stamina to achieve brilliant results in the 1913 road racing season.

In May 1913, O'Shea took a break from serious cycling, after winning the 26-mile Canterbury Championship Road Race. A studied tactician, he followed a strict training regime in the build-up to any major cycling event. He would rest for several weeks before developing a base fitness by taking long walks around the Port Hills behind Christchurch. Only after he was confident that he had developed a strong foundation would he start cycle training in earnest, always timing his training to peak for a specific event.

O'Shea's sights were set on two classic events, both held at the end of the 1913 road season – the Timaru to Christchurch and the Taranaki Round-the-Mountain Road Race, which was the North Island equivalent. For decades, these prestigious events decided the New Zealand champion of the road. The Canterbury course was relatively flat but prone to battering nor'westers. The 100-mile Taranaki epic had a reputation for hills, rain and mud. Winning both would seal O'Shea's position as a champion among champions.

In Taranaki, O'Shea started from scratch against two Australian champions, one being Don Kirkham who had beaten him in the Sydney six-day race. The weather was atrocious and took its toll on them all.

Fourth-placed Arthur Bonis later observed, "It's the hardest race I've ever tackled … the road between

Opunake and Kaponga is bad and takes it out of you. By Jove! Talk about rain, didn't it just pelt down; I never saw anything like it."[21]

However, O'Shea had the bit between his teeth and set a new record for the unsealed century of 5 hours 25 minutes and 15 seconds. As a local paper went on to report, "O'Shea has for some years now proved himself absolutely invincible on the road and is without doubt the best road rider in Australasia. ..."[22]

Back in the South Island a few weeks later, the champion aimed to reinforce the success with a win in the Timaru to Christchurch. He started from scratch, battling Australian competition and the significant difficulties of the course. O'Shea later recalled:

In 1913, we even had to ride on the grass in the middle of the Maronan road because the trees had blown down on the side. ... I suppose that between Timaru and Christchurch we would go through 50 or 60 water races along the way. And then there

O'Shea flies around the outside to win the final of the St. Patrick's Sports Day Wheel Race at Lancaster Park, 1913.

O'Shea Collection

was the Selwyn River. We used to carry our bikes across that. But if the water was too deep we had to climb a barbed wire fence with our bikes and go on over the railway bridge. I was lucky because I never struck a train, either there or at Rakaia. But I remember there were others who did, and they had to hang on for grim death while the train went past.[23]

"I never struck a train, either there or at Rakaia. But I remember there were others who did, and they had to hang on for grim death while the train went past."

At the finish, "All were neck and neck," reported the Christchurch *Press.*

Round the course they came in a heap, and the crowd, becoming excited, leaped the fences and swarmed on to the course. It was with difficulty only that they could be kept back. Fifty yards from home O'Shea, at the right moment shot ahead, with Shalders and Kerr hanging on to his hind wheel. He kept his position, however, and passed the finishing post a wheel ahead of Shalders. ... O'Shea was the hero of the moment, and his excited supporters cheered him to the echo as they carried him to the dressing room.[24]

TRIPLE CROWN

O'Shea had not only won first place and fastest time in the 1913 race, a rare achievement, but also set a new record for the 180 kilometres of 5 hours 14 minutes 58 seconds. At the prize giving:

The crowd cheered heartily, giving three rousing ones for the winner ... then came cries of "Speech! O'Shea, speech!" But O'Shea was understood to say that he would rather ride the course over again than make a speech, and that he was no good at "skite-ing" whereupon he modestly subsided and retired to the region below … [25]

These two key wins in 1913, and numerous victories in smaller events, including an unofficial 10-mile world road record as part of the 100-Mile Dunlop Relay Test (O'Shea's time for 10 miles was 22 minutes 42 seconds), were heralded across the country. His Timaru to Christchurch record was not beaten until 1944, but by this time, the course was 12 miles shorter, much of it was sealed and all the water crossings were gone.

Riders assemble in New Plymouth for the start of the Round-the-Mountain Road Race, circa 1912.

Puke Ariki

THE TIMARU TO CHRISTCHURCH ROAD RACE

Many are called, but few are chosen to survive with distinction in the classic cycling marathon. … For the path of the rider is beset with pitfalls both literally and otherwise. Skill and judgment and luck, also, are needed to overcome them. And the long weary miles sap the reserves of physical energy, calling upon a resolution beaten on the anvil of athletic ambition. The race goes not only to the fleet of wheel, but to the strong of spirit.[26]

The first Timaru to Christchurch Road Race was organised in 1899 (four years before riders pedaled off in the inaugural Tour de France). It is New Zealand's oldest cycle race, and throughout O'Shea's racing career it was the largest and most important, alternating with the Taranaki Round-the-Mountain Road Race for the honour of being the New Zealand Road Championship event. The results from these races determined which cyclists would represent New Zealand in the Australasian Road Racing Championships a few weeks later.

The route used for the Timaru to Christchurch during O'Shea's reign bears little resemblance to the current path of State Highway 1. The course was 180 kilometres long (112 miles) in the early 1900s and followed a hilly route via Arundel. Rocks, stream crossings, mud and the inevitable Canterbury wind took their toll on both man and machine. By 1951, all waterways were safely bridged and racing officials lamented that the course had become "a 100-mile bitumenised speed track".[27]

The Timaru to Christchurch took place near the end of the road racing season (September or October). The handicapped race saw front riders wobbling off at around 9 am, with scratch riders waiting up to 55 minutes for their start. Hundreds of supporters gathered at the towns en route to cheer the riders on, and thousands more waited at the finish line. Progress reports and results were relayed via radio on the day, and newspapers printed full-page features on the event. Often, enthusiastic crowds, unable to contain their excitement, poured onto the course as the winners crossed the finish line.

The great race suffered a hiatus of six years during World War One, returning in all its glory in 1921.

Between 1909 and 1923, O'Shea started nine Timaru to Christchurch races and gained fastest time in six, as well as winning line honours in 1909 and 1913. Punctures put him out of contention in 1910 and 1912. He won in 1909, despite a crash that buckled his rear wheel, and in 1911 he achieved fastest time despite a crash that gashed open his head, resulting in stitches at the finish line.

In 1913, fewer than half of the competitors completed the race, the majority suffering from mechanical mishaps (mostly punctures), crashes or simply from losing motivation when O'Shea passed them earlier than expected. That year, he scorched through with a time of 5 hours 14 minutes 58 seconds – a course record never broken on the 180-kilometre route.

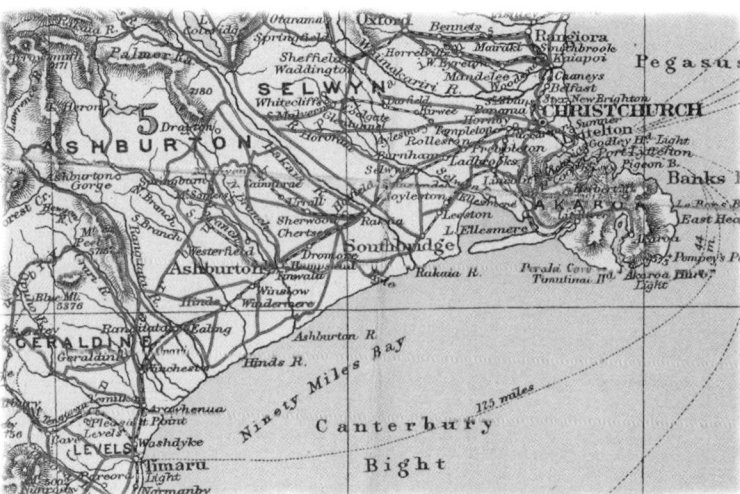

A segment of a 1916 map showing the route from Timaru (south-west) to Christchurch (north-east). No road existed between Hinds and Ashburton, so cyclists were forced to take a hilly inland route.

1916 Bacon Cyclists and Motorists Map, ATL, MapColl-Acc-23668

O'Shea was a rising star in a sport that had a huge following in New Zealand and abroad. He was poised to move to even greater challenges, quietly contemplating an attempt at the Tour de France. But events were to occur that would eclipse all else. In 1914, Britain declared war on Germany and New Zealand leapt to support the 'mother country'; public attention was drawn to the business of war, and O'Shea's thoughts of competing abroad were shelved. He always regretted missing out on the Tour de France.

Two months after the war started, O'Shea again won fastest time in the Timaru to Christchurch, but the numbers of competitors and spectators had dwindled significantly. He continued track racing, and in January 1915, set a New Zealand 1-mile record (2 minutes 15 seconds), but it was obvious there was no longer strong public support for competitive cycling. In December 1915, O'Shea joined the New Zealand armed forces heading for the Great War.

This portrait of Phil O'Shea with his early victories written below was produced as a postcard.

O'Shea Collection

THE BLOODY ROADS OF WAR

Not a bad life, if you can put up with it without cutting your throat.[1]

During the Great War of 1914–1918, New Zealand raised 110,368 troops to defend the Empire and help conquer the invading forces of Germany.[2] On 15 December 1915, Phil O'Shea added his name to the list of young men volunteering for active service "for the duration of war". He was 25 years old.

Little is known of O'Shea's war years. For his generation, it was a topic rarely broached. We can only assume he used the same quiet attentiveness that made him a tactical master of cycle racing to keep his head down and survive.

O'Shea completed a military medical examination in September 1915, then waited two months for his call-up to service. Recruiting for the New Zealand Expeditionary Force was still voluntary, but passions ran high and local recruiting committees did such a good job that numbers applying consistently exceeded needs. The government had a 'concentration' policy to prevent a volunteer from entering training camp until required, providing time for the volunteer, and more importantly their civilian workplace, to adjust to the loss of yet another able-bodied young man from civilian life.[3]

Phil and Elizabeth O'Shea's
wedding portrait.

O'Shea Collection

In November 1915, O'Shea received word to proceed to the preliminary training camp in Trentham, Upper Hutt, for five weeks. From there, he went by rail to the new Featherston training camp, which accommodated 7,500 men – 4,500 in huts and 3,000 under canvas. Did O'Shea pass his nights there under the flapping of heavy canvas? There are no records to tell us, but, whatever the case, he must have remembered even those cramped quarters with nostalgia in the months to follow.

The end of eight weeks of intensive training was marked with a 50-kilometre march over the Rimutaka Mountain Road back to Trentham, before O'Shea took leave to prepare for departure. As part of that preparation, on 9 March 1916, he married his sweetheart Elizabeth Graham, a 24-year-old dressmaker from Amberley.

A few weeks later, on 1 April 1916, as a recruit of the New Zealand Army Service Corps (NZASC) 11th Reinforcements, O'Shea set sail for Suez in Egypt. His rank was driver in mechanical transport of the No. 1 Field Ambulance.

Within a month of arriving in Egypt, O'Shea found himself

marching north to Alexandria to board ship once again, this time bound for England on a slow and dangerous journey.

> Every precaution was taken against submarines. No lights were allowed on deck between sunset and reveille, and all lights below were carefully shaded and deadlights closed. The minimum of noise was enjoined after dark. All ranks worked, ate and slept in lifebelts ... [4]

At Sling, in the heart of the Salisbury Plains of England, was New Zealand's chief training camp. Here the soldiers re-trained in drill and musketry, range practice, wiring and throwing bombs, gas-mask drill (including visits to the gas chamber), Lewis gun use, mock attacks and trench digging. O'Shea's skills were honed, his courage was tested and, after 30 days of rigorous training, he was deemed ready to join battle in France. The reality involved little battling and long, forgettable stretches of drudgery.

The reality involved little battling and long, forgettable stretches of drudgery.

> So it's push along, get along,
> Column of route from the right.
> Leather soft, wagons clean,
> Pole chains shining bright.
> Doing work for everyone, foot and cavalree –
> Jack of every bloomin' trade –
> N–Z–A–S–C.[5]

With no account from O'Shea, his role in the ensuing fighting can only be pieced together by matching his war records with official published accounts of the time. He served with the regiment of the NZASC

No. 1 Field Ambulance from July 1916, proceeding first to Etaples and then Rouen in northern France, to join the push for the western front. Initially taking the role of despatch rider, O'Shea was later to become ambulance car driver, and his rank changed

In 1916, when O'Shea was a despatch rider, motorbikes were essentially bicycles with motors added.

ATL, Jones Collection, G-25963-1/2

to 'artificer' (military mechanic). In the sea of mud and disarray, his mechanical skills and unflappable temperament would doubtless have been crucial. As one report states, "The roads were one solid mass of traffic – wagons, guns, limbers, tractors, lorries – and flashing in and out among them all, the motorcycles of the despatch riders."[6]

O'Shea was involved in battles in France, similar to the following, which took place in July 1916:

The motor ambulance drivers did good work steering their cars through the town [Armentières] in the height of the bombardment, houses crashing to the ground in every street during the two hours the action covered. ... Great difficulty was experienced in getting the stretcher cases out owing to blockage of the communications trenches by shell fire and the debris in the streets of the town, which the cars had to avoid as best they could. ... raids followed in rapid succession, gas, smoke and shells were floated or hurled towards the enemy's lines; he not to be outdone in animosity returned in kind.[7]

An advanced dressing station on the Somme during World War One.

ATL, RSA Collection, G-12928-1/2

As the battalions pressed on from Armentières towards Flers, chaos reigned. Heavy rain set in, turning simple dirt lanes into seething mires. Many side routes had to be abandoned, and all transport converged on the main metalled thoroughfares. The pace on the now congested main routes slowed to a crawl, with field ambulances covering an average of four kilometres an hour. The conditions may have been frustrating and dangerous, but still the soldiers' optimism remained high:

> Apart from the strain of being under shell fire and the danger attached thereto, the life is much easier

O'Shea's rank as artificer required him to repair military vehicles as well as drive them. Here a group of New Zealand artificers is shown working at what was called "the cars hospital".

ATL, G-12889-1/2

than what I have been used to up country. Food
is good. Breakfast, cold bacon; dinner, bully beef;
tea, stew or potted meat and potatoes.[8]

Around this time, General Godley decided the troops
needed healthy outdoor entertainment to boost
morale. He instigated and encouraged "recreational
training" that took the form of many sporting
matches between teams of men, including football
– something a sportsman like O'Shea must have
revelled in.

In the downtime between fighting, O'Shea took
part in sunbathing, delousing and letter writing, as
well as sports. Also, twice in the three years and 39
days he served overseas, O'Shea was given relief from
the war front to take two weeks' leave to the United
Kingdom.

On one of his periods of leave, O'Shea made a
trip to Ireland to meet with relatives he had never
seen. It proved eventful. At this time, Ireland was
fiercely independent and disdained anything British.
A naïve O'Shea arrived at the arranged pub kitted
out in the military overcoat and uniform supplied to
all New Zealand recruits, compliments of the British
Army. As he entered, a silence fell on the room. One
by one all stood and walked out past the bewildered
O'Shea. Devastated, he decided to cut short his visit
and return to London. Luckily, some of his female
relatives stepped in to resolve the misunderstanding,
and O'Shea met his relatives later that week.

Back once more in active service, O'Shea found
himself moving slowly across France and into Belgium,

He had spent nearly three years driving to and from the front, over muddy, crater-riddled roads, sometimes at night without lights on.

taking in action at Somme and Passchendaele along the way. Somehow he managed to avoid the influenza epidemic that swept the troops, claiming many lives in October 1918, but encounters with mustard gas left him with "a sore chest from a bit of gas". From his military service record, we know that on 1 March 1919 he was admitted to a hospital at Maryhill in Scotland for a week. He had spent nearly three years driving to and from the front, over muddy, crater-riddled roads, sometimes at night without lights on. His cargo was broken bodies. He took the live ones, but saw plenty of dead left behind. He never lost his hatred of Germans, fuelled by experiences such as discovering a group of New Zealanders lying on the side of the road, shot in the back of the head. Like many soldiers in World War One, his nerves suffered from chronic exposure to such barbarity.

On 27 March 1919, Phil O'Shea returned to New Zealand with 979 others on the *SS Kia Ora* to pick up the pieces of his life. Although O'Shea still suffered from the horrors experienced in Europe, he never spoke of them publicly. He quickly saw that he needed to move on, so he did the only thing he could with skill and confidence. He eventually got back on his bike and started riding again.

O'Shea served in France
and Belgium, where
this photo was taken in
December 1917 showing
"Wintry conditions at the
New Zealand Headquarters"
Château Segard.

ATL, RSA Collection, G- 1809-10x8

BACK IN THE SADDLE

> When I returned to New Zealand in 1919, I had
> no intention of riding again. I was over-weight,
> nervy, and a bit burnt-out, yet I was not yet 30
> years old.[1]

Phil O'Shea was finally released from army service in
June 1919. He spent that winter quietly recuperating –
but ultimately could not resist the pull of cycle racing.
Later he admitted, "Watching a few races, a sense of
competition prompted me to mount again to find out
if the young fellows were as good as they looked."[2]
Four years had passed since O'Shea's last race, but on
his return he took to training with more dedication
than ever, commencing daily breathing exercises to
increase the capacity of his gas-damaged lungs. His
pre-war medical examination recorded O'Shea as
having a chest expansion of 12.5 centimetres[3] – the
average is 8 centimetres.

O'Shea built himself up slowly and methodically
for his return to cycling, training without strain and
entering short races in which he was usually beaten.
But the potential was there, and by the end of the
year, it was realised.

> In the Christmas and New Year holidays of
> 1919/1920 I went up to Gisborne [for the national
> track championships], fitter than I had been for

years. Successes there put me on my feet. I won
five races, all track championships bar one.[4]

In such a tactical sport as track racing, O'Shea had the
advantage of experience and confidence and, at the
age of 30, he was just reaching his physical peak. The
fact that almost all the riders he lined up against were
considerably younger bears testimony to the time.
Dozens of champion athletes, including O'Shea's
hero Jack Arnst, had been killed in World War One,
and many more maimed. But if competition were
lacking, cycling handicappers quickly adjusted the
starts to ensure the champion would struggle for line
honours.

After returning to top form on the track, O'Shea
hit the road like a hurricane. In the spring of 1920,
the Athletics, Axemen's and Cycling Union held a
70-mile New Zealand Championship race across
the Canterbury Plains. The wiry veteran started on
scratch – alone. His handicap was a daunting 40 minutes behind the first bunch of riders, but he took up
the challenge with style and finished in second place
with fastest time.

Many more wins on track and road followed.
O'Shea became a household name and a wealthy man.
By this stage, he was sponsored by Speedy Cycles and
winning prize money in virtually every race he entered. The owner of Speedy Cycles, Jack Suckling,
also owned a motorcar business, where he employed
O'Shea as mechanic before and after the war.

In 1921, the famous Timaru to Christchurch Road
Race was resurrected. "The Wonder Wheelman"

*O'Shea became a
household name and
a wealthy man.*

stamped his mark by gaining fastest time, an achievement he was to repeat the following year, finishing
a full 20 minutes ahead of the second fastest time.
With such success conclusive evidence of his stand-
ing in New Zealand cycling, O'Shea was officially
selected once more to represent New Zealand in the
Australasian Road Racing Championship of 1922.
The event was the 265-kilometre Warrnambool to
Melbourne, which had not been held since O'Shea's
last win in 1911.

Speedy Cycles supported
many top cyclists. O'Shea
is in the front row, second
from the right.

ATI, Adam Maclay Collection,
G-24016-1/1

"What makes his feats all the more remarkable is that after having outstanding victories in New Zealand and Australia, he did not race between 1915 and 1918 as he was serving with the New Zealand forces in the First World War ..."[6]

Well before the race started, the New Zealand riders found themselves challenged. O'Shea recalled: "It used to take us three days and four nights to come from New Zealand on the boat. I don't know which was the worst — the bike race or the boat ride."[5] Despite the tiring journey across the Tasman, the race was a coup for New Zealand cycling. First across the line was Peter Hill from Christchurch, with O'Shea winning fastest time once again. O'Shea was the only rider out of 200 starters to complete the distance in under nine hours (8 hours 59 minutes).

Twenty years later, Harry James from the Dunlop Rubber Company (title sponsor of the Warrnambool to Melbourne) recalled the sensational finish: "… despite the presence of additional police, [Hill and O'Shea] were mobbed by thousands as they rode to the post at the Ascot racecourse. Pickets cracked as the mob surged forward to carry the visitors shoulder high."[7]

Some claimed the wins were nothing more than luck for Hill and O'Shea, the two riders benefiting from others' misfortunes. The rising star of Australian cycling, Hubert Opperman, had been rated a strong contender before the race but lost any chance of winning when he punctured, although he still managed to finish with fourth fastest time.

In his autobiography, Opperman described how the leading bunch misjudged the final turn into the Ascot racecourse, with dramatic consequences:

Eleven minutes ahead a big bunch made a cavalry charge to the sharply angled right hand turn.

Brakeless, they crashed into a piled-up discord of defeat. Peter Hill, of New Zealand, wearily well in the rear, now warily steered though the bruised bodies, buckled wheels and scraping pedals to the plaudits of a crowd still dripping from fire hoses turned on to cool down a feverish excitement, which threatened to engulf the track.[8]

Opperman's admiration for "the brilliant all-round New Zealander, Phil O'Shea ... " was also clearly expressed in his memoirs:

> O'Shea's short, 5ft. 6in. excellently proportioned body was richly endowed for all distances, as a top-ranking track sprinter he could summon up from the depths of versatile capacity a beautifully timed second jump for the line, at the end of the longest race.[9]

Riding through the infamous Stony Rises – a 30-kilometre rolling climb – on the 1922 Warrnambool to Melbourne Road Race.
O'Shea Collection

O'SHEA'S SPEEDY STEEDS

"My bike rode as sweet as a lollie,"[10] O'Shea would say after finishing a race with no mechanical problems. Early 1900s roads were treacherous: "Naturally there were far more punctures because roads in those days were repaired with broken metal. All right for drays, but not for bikes. We all rode with heavier tyres," O'Shea later recalled.[11]

O'Shea rode a top-of-the-line Speedy racing bicycle until the mid-1920s, when he switched to a Jones Special. Both bikes were custom-made in Christchurch. The frame and most components were made of steel. The bikes had a single fixed gear (with no freewheel) – and no brakes! At 28 pounds (12.7 kilograms), O'Shea's Speedy bicycle was lightweight for the times. On the track, O'Shea used wooden rims with lightweight tubular tyres and a 92-inch gear. For road work, his wheels had strong steel rims and heavy puncture-resistant clincher tyres (28 inches by $1^3/_8$ inches).

In the 1911 Warrnambool to Melbourne, O'Shea apparently stated that his bike had an 89-inch gear and 7-inch (178 millimetre) cranks.[12] Was this possible? It is the equivalent of a 53-tooth chainwheel and a 16-tooth cog. Was O'Shea strong enough to push that gear up the Stony Rises, a gradual hill over 30 kilometres long? Gear selection was crucial for long road races and varied with the course and weather conditions. Considering O'Shea's great race record, it is unlikely he ever made a major error in gear selection.

Carbon fibre, titanium and aluminium have now mostly replaced steel, and the weights of road bikes have plummeted to 7.5 kilograms or less. Front and rear brakes are mandatory on the road, and 20 gears are common.

It is difficult to estimate the difference in speed between racing bikes from 1910 and 2005. Ten per cent is a conservative estimate. O'Shea himself believed the lightweight wheels used in the 1960s made a difference of perhaps eight kilometres an hour, but they would never have lasted on the treacherous roads or lumpy grass tracks that challenged racers of O'Shea's era.

For his own part, after the race the 33-year-old O'Shea commented, "I seemed to be wearing well. My system of steady training, early to bed and so on, stood me in good stead. But it was not all easy going."[13]

O'Shea was full of praise for New Zealand's other entrant in the race, Dan Wright, who finished a valiant sixth. "[Wright] toed it in like a madman all the way ... he rode a great race. ... He was placed fifth but in reality got fourth."[14]

In 1923, despite excellent training and a wealth of experience, Phil had his hardest year of road racing. The younger generation of riders had come of age, and O'Shea was to line up against two great cyclists that year − future New Zealand champion Harry Watson and Australian star Opperman. However, O'Shea had one advantage over his two younger rivals: his phenomenal finishing kick. By 1923, he was virtually unbeatable on distances from one to 10 miles. He was the 1923 New Zealand 1-, 2- and 3-mile track champion and easily transferred that sprinting skill to road racing.

With stunning bursts of speed, O'Shea would power from scratch in a long-distance road race and work his way through the field by hopping from one bunch to the next. Upon catching a group of riders, he would often ride straight to the front to let all know that he had arrived still feeling strong. Then, drifting to the back, he would sit in behind and catch his breath before taking off again to catch the next bunch. The benefits of psychological tactics were not

With stunning bursts of speed, O'Shea would power from scratch in a long-distance road race and work his way through the field by hopping from one bunch to the next.

lost on the champion. If any scratch riders managed to stick with him to the end, one or two carefully timed sprints would soon dispose of them.

The 1923 Timaru to Christchurch Road Championship proved to be the most gruelling race in O'Shea's career. A week before, he was dangerously ill with influenza and running a temperature of 103°F (39.5°C), but he was determined to win in order to represent New Zealand, once again, in the upcoming Australasian championship.

On race day, 29 September, competitors were greeted by a stiflingly hot, energy-sapping nor'west headwind. On the start line outside the Grand Hotel in Timaru, however, O'Shea felt fine.

Just before 10 am, 52 minutes after the first riders had left, the three scratchmen, O'Shea, Hill and Wright, set off northwards. They rode together but even before reaching Temuka at the 20-kilometre mark, O'Shea was in agony. It was obvious now that his recovery had been superficial and, in a weakened state, he was having difficulties he had never experienced before. Only as they passed through Rakaia did O'Shea finally manage to rouse his iron determination and struggle his way, inch by painful inch, ahead of his rivals.

At Selwyn, however, just over 30 kilometres from the finish, O'Shea crashed while crossing the rocky river bed. He surrendered to his illness and lay down exhausted. Then, alone on the river bed, he gave himself the 'coach talk' that convinced him to continue – and ultimately clinch his status as New

Zealand's greatest cyclist: "You are a champion: people expect more of champions," he chided himself. Hauling himself back on the bike, his face a pasty white and with wobbly legs, he battled on.

An expectant 3,000-strong crowd roared as O'Shea slogged his way across the finish line and fell off his bike. Supporters rushed to carry him away on their shoulders. Everyone wanted to touch the hero. O'Shea had finished the race in 12th place, but once again, for the sixth time in his career, with fastest

O'Shea after the tortuous Timaru to Christchurch Road Race.

O'Shea Collection

The New Zealand public honestly and passionately believed that Phil O'Shea was unbeatable.

"They were out to knobble me."

time. At the awards function, officials heralded him as "the best road and track rider in the world today".[15] Such an enthusiastic exaggeration demonstrates not only how insular New Zealand was at the time but also in what high regard O'Shea was held – the New Zealand public honestly and passionately believed that Phil O'Shea was unbeatable.

First across the line, with second fastest time, only 10 minutes slower than O'Shea's 6 hours 50 seconds, was the young Harry Watson.

THE WARRNAMBOOL TO MELBOURNE HAT TRICK

By 1923, the Australian wheelmen had had enough of being beaten by Kiwis, especially O'Shea, who wore his silver fern with ardent pride. As well as patriotism, there was £50 prize money at stake in the Warrnambool to Melbourne. But rumours travel fast, and O'Shea later recounted that before the race he suspected "they were out to knobble me".[16] His solution was to disappear.

First, O'Shea put his race number upside down on his back. Then, during the race, he happily allowed mud and dust to further obscure his identity. Some distance along the course, disguise complete, he quietly slipped up to a large bunch and heard them talking:

"Has O'Shea come through yet?"

"No."

"Well, you go on, and we'll hold him back."

O'Shea nudged his feed bag across to further

obscure his race number before working his way quietly up through the malignant bunch. Just as he glided off the front, someone yelled out, "Hey, is that O'Shea's number?" Before they had time to figure it out, O'Shea was gone. Decades later, O'Shea would advise his grandson, "Never trust those Aussies."

This was another unlucky year for Hubert Opperman. Much of the 265-kilometre course was in terrible condition, and he punctured again, yet was still only three minutes off the fastest time at the finish. O'Shea also punctured 20 miles from the finish, but his was a slow leak and, as he was neck and neck with another scratchman, J. Beasley, he dared

The New Zealand competitors in the 1923 Warrnambool to Melbourne Road Race (left to right) O'Shea, Charlie Bell and Harry Watson.

O'Shea Collection

Passing cyclists are given hot bread and milk during the 1922 Warrnambool to Melbourne Road Race.

O'Shea Collection

No one had ever claimed a hat-trick of fastest times before.

not stop to replace the tube. He rode off the saddle for the last six miles and just managed to sprint to victory, winning by less than a second.

"I seldom get excited, but I was proud of that," O'Shea recalled. "By hell it was a long way to ride a bike." O'Shea's win was proof for any who still needed it that he was the most outstanding cyclist riding in New Zealand and Australia. No one had ever claimed a hat-trick of fastest times before. Opperman was to manage three championship wins over the next six years, but O'Shea's victories followed in convincing succession and were seemingly unaffected by the 10-year hiatus for the race.

Shortly after the 1923 Warrnambool to Melbourne, O'Shea announced his retirement from road racing. *The Press* reflected soberly: "This will be regretted by all interested in road racing, for Phil O'Shea will be greatly missed from the classic road events."[17] True as this may have been, the announcement must also have come as a relief to some of O'Shea's cycling rivals.

By this stage, Phil O'Shea had a one-year-old daughter, Doreen. Perhaps the long absences from his family for training and travelling were proving too demanding. Certainly, O'Shea did not deny that his supreme effort in that year's Timaru to Christchurch had taken its toll: "I may get in two or three more seasons on the track, but another road season would kill me."[18]

Phil O'Shea with his wife, Elizabeth, and daughter, Doreen.

O'Shea Collection

WHIRLWIND ON WHEELS

In the early 1900s, cycle racing tracks were built in most New Zealand cities and towns. They dotted Canterbury – the epicentre of cycling – like craters on the moon. Most were laid on grass or cinders (crushed coke), but one stood out for its size and location, as well as its asphalted surface. Lancaster Park in Christchurch was the scene of many memorable cycling events, including the 1887 visit by Fred Wood, World Penny Farthing Champion, New Zealand's first women's track cycling race in 1896 and the 1903 victory of New Zealand Champion George Sutherland over former World Sprint Champion Marshall 'Major' Taylor of the United States. (Major Taylor won the World Sprint title in 1899. He was a staunch Methodist who refused to race on Sundays. An African American, he felt pressure from racism at home and pursued his career further afield, mostly in Europe and Australasia.) A crowd of 8,000 had gathered to witness Sutherland's spectacular win.

Phil O'Shea served his track apprenticeship at Lancaster Park. He often raced there and later reminisced:

> In 1910 and 1911 I rode scores of times on the old
> asphalt track at Lancaster Park. The first time there,
> I won a wheel race and two days later ran third

English park april 5.th 1924

The start of the 10-mile track championship, English Park Stadium, Christchurch, April 1924.

O'Shea Collection

in two New Zealand track championships. There were big crowds, and it was great sport.[1]

During the First World War, however, the track was ripped up to make way for a community vegetable garden. While this dealt a major blow to track racing in Christchurch, it did not stop O'Shea. On his return from war service, he travelled regularly around the country to compete in track events, with consistent success. Between 1920 and 1924, he claimed more than a dozen New Zealand track championships, while ostensibly concentrating his efforts on the road!

In 1924, a new asphalt track opened at English Park Stadium in Christchurch. The ex-champion George Sutherland was employed to promote the stadium, and he promptly contracted New Zealand's most famous cyclist to race there. In the 1924–25 track season, O'Shea appeared at two meetings a week at English Park. He lost just one race off the scratch mark.[2] At the 1924 National Track Championships hosted at the park, O'Shea cleaned up, winning the ½-mile, 1-mile, 2-mile and 3-mile medals.

Sutherland, meanwhile, had not been resting on his laurels. Spectator interest meant everything to the success of the stadium, which earned its keep solely through admission charges. Sutherland sought to capitalise on support for the golden boy of New Zealand cycling by arranging a series of match races. These were similar to the match competitions found in boxing, with O'Shea lining up against national and international cycling stars to race for considerable sums of money (each athlete earned up to £100 appearance money and the winner another £50). The best out of three races would decide the match winner.

O'Shea's first opponent was an enthusiastic young local by the name of Bill Mackie. He was the New Zealand Motor-Paced Champion and had it in mind to take O'Shea's spot in the limelight. In late February 1925, the two lined up at English Park Stadium in front of a record crowd of 8,000 people. Mackie was out of his depth, beaten convincingly by the champion – first in a ¼-mile unpaced race and then in a 3-mile paced event. O'Shea won the latter in 6 minutes 30 seconds.

Soon the promoter had to look further afield for exciting competition to maintain public interest, and in March 1925, the great Willie Spencer, 1923 United States Cycling Champion, was shipped over for a match race.

The result was pandemonium. Never had there been such a crowd at English Park. The stadium had an official capacity of 10,000 and was cram-packed that evening. "Hundreds more were clamouring at the gates for admission, but in vain."[3]

The two champions lined up for the first race — the ¼-mile unpaced.

> As the roar of the spectators announced the progress of the race, those gathered outside the back entrance lifted the gates off their hinges and surged in to the already overcrowded grounds. The fence at the back of the stadium, which was topped with barbed-wire, was treated with contempt by many fans, who climbed up to the top and hung on by the posts. Before 9 o'clock, there was a sensation in the back seats. Some of the posts gave way, and those who were depending on their support tumbled down into the packed seats.[4]

It is clear from newspaper reports that the audience did not comprehend the tactics being played out before them.

> As soon as the riders left the mark they adopted the 'go slow policy', one watching the other as a cat watches a mouse. Sections of the crowd commenced

to hoot and cry out, 'Call them off.' Evidently they did not understand that the race was being run on Continental lines, where a rider matches his brains as well as his ability to pedal with those of his opponent.[5]

On the back straight, O'Shea jumped. The crowd roared as "the big Yank" set after him. This was racing as they had never seen it before. "From the time the riders entered the [back] straight until some minutes after the finish the crowd opened its collective mouth and simply bellowed with excitement." With a magnificent burst of acceleration, Spencer gave chase and caught O'Shea, and the pair wrestled each other for line honours. When the announcer could finally be heard to say, "O'Shea first", another thunderclap of cheering swept through the stadium. The winning margin was only a few inches.

A 1-mile paced race came next. From the start, Spencer tucked in behind the pacer, while O'Shea sat in the rear for the first three laps. In the final lap, the pacer rode off ahead as Spencer slowed down to offer a reluctant O'Shea the lead. The offer was declined. Finally, in the back stretch, Spencer set sail, opening a small gap. O'Shea wound it up on the bend, climbing high in an attempt to pass his rival on the outside, but suddenly crashed. Spencer slackened his pace and crossed the line to the booing of thousands. Angry spectators accused the American of knocking into O'Shea's front wheel, while others claimed the local hero simply lost traction and skidded into the fence. Whatever the cause, O'Shea was taken to hospital

O'Shea wound it up on the bend, climbing high in an attempt to pass his rival on the outside, but suddenly crashed ...

With his arms in bandages, O'Shea lines up against United States Champion Willie Spencer at Athletic Park, Wellington, March 1925.

O'Shea Collection

and, after having his wounds cleaned, was declared unfit for further racing that night.

A week later, the pair met again, this time in Wellington on the football field at Athletic Park. Willie Spencer, who was used to racing on smooth board tracks, stood aghast when he saw what he was required to race on. He asked if anyone present had a camera, as he had "never raced on a lawn"[6] and would like a photo to show cyclists back in America.

The race, another ¼-mile, once again ended in disaster. O'Shea went with the flash of the gun and took the lead from the start (an advantage on an unbanked

LILY WHITES AND THE FILTHY LUCRE

A bitter debate between 'amateur' and 'cash' cycling raged throughout O'Shea's childhood. By the time he started racing, it had been lost by the 'lily whites' (amateurs) and all the major cycling events in Australasia were 'cash' events.

Cash cycling, later called professional cycling, offered money as prizes. Amateur cycling officials believed that accepting the 'filthy lucre' was immoral. Although O'Shea never got involved in the public debate (he later coached both amateurs and 'pros'), privately he felt that if he "bust a gut" racing, he deserved to win some prize money. It was simply a practical means of paying for the tools of his sport and later earning a living.

O'Shea was also a patriotic Kiwi. He could represent New Zealand by travelling to Australia and racing for 'cash and country'. During his career, northern hemisphere events such as the Tour de France (professional) and Olympic Games (mostly amateur) barely rated a mention down under.

In 1930, the inaugural Empire Games (later called the Commonwealth Games) also gave cyclists an opportunity to represent New Zealand, but only as amateurs. This stipulation boosted the revival of amateur cycling for several decades. The two branches – amateurs and professionals – were finally amalgamated in 1994. However, there is less opportunity for riders to earn a living from cycling in New Zealand today than in the 1920s, when O'Shea and other top riders earned the average income or better on the local cash circuit. These days, professional Kiwi cyclists must race overseas to earn a living.

grass track as it is difficult to pass on the outside). Spencer built up too much speed trying to pass on the bend and crashed into the crowd. O'Shea looked back to see what had happened to his rival and also crashed, tearing the bandages off his arms and ending up in hospital, this time for six weeks. The match was a fiasco and made for a sour end to an otherwise fantastic track season for O'Shea. Although it highlighted the difficulty of racing at top speed around a football field, the "renowned mud-slinging newspaper" *Truth* used it as an opportunity to pan professional cyclists. This incensed professional rider and North Island Champion Dave Nicholson, who wrote to *Truth* and challenged any amateur cyclist to a match race. *Truth* retorted that amateurs were not permitted to race against professionals and told Nicholson to "bury his head in the sands of Castlecliff".[7]

At the beginning of 1926, *The Christchurch Sun* newspaper reported that O'Shea was racing well below par. Commenting on one mid-January race set at English Park Stadium, the reporter noted:

> New Zealand's greatest cyclist certainly looked as if he had hit the toboggan that ends all athletes who hang on too long. He has toiled like a Trojan in amassing the huge list of performances that proclaims him the best cyclist New Zealand has ever produced and one of the greatest all-rounders the world has known. But the writing on the wall is plain, and the idol of New Zealand cycling enthusiasts is nearing the end of his wonderful innings.[8]

"He has toiled like a Trojan in amassing the huge list of performances that proclaims him the best cyclist New Zealand has ever produced ..."

In the mid 1920s, groups of Christchurch riders would travel together to do a track circuit around the South Island. O'Shea is in the middle, sitting on the running board, with his racing mate Jack Henderson on his right.

Ray Henderson Collection

Phil O'Shea and Jack Henderson in front of a group at their track-side campsite, circa 1920s.

Ray Henderson Collection

Despite this gloomy prediction, or perhaps because of it, O'Shea filled his calendar for 1926 with another rigorous season of track racing. He was matched against Australian H.W. Nesbitt and prominent New Zealanders, Fred 'Jumbo' Wells and Bill Mackie (his arch-rival). He beat them all.

Sutherland, ever the consummate promoter, then brought in the Australian Champion, Harris Horder (later to become United States Sprint Champion). With skilful advertising and wide reporting, Sutherland used the star billing to attract a crowd of 7,000 paying spectators to the opening of the

A massive crowd watches the final of the Timaru Wheel Race, won by Phil O'Shea, circa 1926.

O'Shea Collection

Blandford Park Stadium in Auckland on 8 March 1926. The pair had sized each other up a few days earlier when Horder beat O'Shea in a match race at English Park Stadium in Christchurch. In Auckland, the tables were turned.

In the first race, the ½-mile paced, Horder was leading by a length when he crashed on the bend. O'Shea had to swerve hard to avoid him but made it to the finish unscathed. To the relief of the crowd, Horder got up and walked back to the pavilion.

Phil O'Shea, Harris Horder and their managers are photographed before the Auckland race disaster.

O'Shea Collection

In the second race, the 1-mile open, the Australian won in a respectable time of 2 minutes 10 seconds.

By the third and final race, Horder's ankle had begun to swell, and he limped to the mark to line up beside O'Shea. The pair raced together to the final bend, where Horder drew ahead before crashing again. This time, O'Shea could not avoid him. Both crashed heavily and had to be helped from the track. Horder was taken to hospital with a suspected broken foot. O'Shea, with typical tenacity, appeared later in the evening for another race.[9]

After a winter of recuperation, O'Shea started the next track season with an even more disastrous race at the 1926 Labour Day races in Ashburton. He had just ridden "to a brilliant finish, winning the 1-mile invitation scratch race"[10] when one of his tyres blew out and he was thrown onto the asphalt track. He was "removed from the track" with a compound fracture of the left collarbone and abrasions to his arms, hand and scalp. This put him out of racing for the rest of the year.

1927 – MACKIE AND SPEARS

In January 1927, after training on rollers, Phil O'Shea made a rapid re-entry into the track racing arena. At the start of February, a new stadium and grass track opened at Monica Park, Christchurch, with the star attraction a match race between O'Shea and Bill Mackie. As usual, the best out of three races won the match – and this time £50. By this stage, O'Shea must have seemed the underdog: he was approaching

40 years of age and had not raced for months. Still, the public loved him and were anxious about his chances. Mackie had made the most of O'Shea's absence, winning many races and retaining the New Zealand motor-pace title.

O'Shea was undaunted. In the first race (½-mile, paced), the matched pair collided in the final lap, and Mackie's wooden front wheel shattered as he hit the deck. Viewing a victory in such circumstances as unsporting, O'Shea declined to cross the finish, and the race was held again. Mackie won the re-run, as O'Shea was unable to get around him on the bends.

In the second race (¾-mile), Mackie took the lead again, but O'Shea got past him on the inside and won. Mackie raised a protest, but this was dismissed.

With the tally set at one win apiece, the riders lined up for the decider. This time, O'Shea leapt to the lead. Mackie tried but failed to pass on the bend, leaving the two to sprint it out on the straight. Again, O'Shea flashed across the line first. "So high did the enthusiasm run that after the race the crowd invaded the field and carried O'Shea off on their shoulders."[11]

A few days later, O'Shea met the Australian Champion (and 1920 World Sprint Champion) Bob Spears. The local hero had the advantage as they were to race at the grassed Monica Park. Spears had never raced on grass before and was easily disposed of in the first two heats. Conceding that O'Shea was the better rider on grass, Spears threw down the gauntlet and challenged O'Shea "to race him on any banked

With the tally set at one win apiece, the riders lined up for the decider ...

Son of an Australian sheep farmer, Bob Spears was the World Sprint Champion in 1920, and runner up in 1921 and 1922. "He trained little, spending most of his time on introducing his friends in throwing the boomerang. ..."[13]

[hard] track in the Dominion."[12] O'Shea accepted, and arrangements were made for them to meet at English Park the following Wednesday.

This time, O'Shea was to get a taste of his own medicine. Each race was a terrific battle: Spears won every one by less than a wheel. Later in the evening, O'Shea consoled himself by winning a 2-mile, tandem-paced scratch race against the local cracks, including Bill Mackie.

THE RECORD BREAKER

By 1927, the papers had been predicting O'Shea's retirement for over a year, but dousing his competitive fire proved difficult. On 19 March, O'Shea lined

Action on the track at Ashburton, circa 1928.

Canterbury Museum

up for the main event of the St. Patrick's Sports Day meeting at English Park. It was his specialty the 1-mile and he was starting from scratch, giving considerable handicaps to local wheelmen. With utter determination, O'Shea wound his machine up until it was flying. He rode possibly the best track race of his life, hauling in the competition and flashing across the line in a new national record time of 2 minutes 1 second. (With the speed he had that day, he could have ridden a kilometre in under 1 minute 15 seconds.) The record was never broken on the old English Park track, by either cash or amateur riders.

With increasing age and competition improving, the following two years were hard for the champion. He continued to make appearances around the country, for special events such as the Athletic Carnival in Auckland and to compete in the national track championships. In 1928, he was the New Zealand 2-mile and 5-mile track champion and came second in the 1-mile and ¼-mile, making him the all-round New Zealand Track Champion. In 1929, he won the ¼-mile track championship title and came second in the 1-mile (one of the few times O'Shea ever made a protest, claiming he was boxed in). Although he was then 40 years old, he still had one great match race to ride. At the end of 1929, the Australian cycling legend Hubert Opperman arrived in New Zealand.

Opperman was by now a world-class cyclist and in top form. Credited with many long-distance road records and road racing titles, he was also a champion motor-pace rider. The previous year, Opperman and

New Zealander Harry Watson had ridden together in the Tour de France, finishing 18th and 28th overall. O'Shea had faced Opperman in the 1922 and 1923 Warrnambool to Melbourne road races and both times snatched victory – the two legends held each other in the highest regard. *The Press* commented, "Opperman's meetings with Watson and O'Shea and his motor-paced riding should be an education to New Zealand cyclists."[14]

As a long-distance rider, Opperman was not to compete in any event less than five miles long in New Zealand. Although he was at the peak of his sporting career, the young Australian was quick to defend his rival against the common speculation that age would defeat O'Shea. "There are still many cyclists winning races ... whose ages are well over 40 years," he stated in an interview with *The Press*. "With the exception of wrestling, cycling allows a man to continue for more years than does any other sport."[15]

The first two races were held on 19 December 1929. The rivals won one apiece. Public interest was primed to fever pitch for the decider at English Park Stadium on 6 January 1930. Several thousand spectators were perched on the edge of their seats as the two scorchers lined up for a 5-mile, tandem-paced finale. Had it been a time trial Opperman would doubtless have won. But tandem-paced races require careful judgement and cunning tactics. O'Shea was a master of both.

Under the headline "Crowd Cheers Frantically as Local Rider Leads Way Home", *The Christchurch Sun*

of 7 January 1930 waxed lyrical over O'Shea's win:

> The final match race between Opperman and O'Shea resulted in a triumphant victory for the Christchurch rider, Opperman being beaten in a stirring race, every minute of which was intensely exciting. The veteran champion O'Shea was never seen in better form, and he was accorded generous applause when he rode home a winner in one of the greatest events of his career. It was a truly outstanding performance and one that will linger long in the memory of lovers of the cycling sport.

Phil O'Shea's (left) last great race was against Australian Hubert Opperman (centre) in January 1930. Harry Watson (right) also raced against Opperman.

Watson Collection

That was Phil O'Shea's last notable match race. Later that year, he won his twenty-second track championship – the ¼-mile. His determination proved as strong as ever when, after crashing badly during another race at the same meeting, he was bandaged up and returned to win a 1-mile scratch race before being admitted to hospital.

But time was running out for the doyen of the track.

"An athlete must know himself how much training he can do … how much he can stand," stated O'Shea.[17] The champion had ridden a phenomenal number of races on road and track over a period of 20 hard and exhilarating years. Finally, O'Shea acknowledged his tired body. He decided it was time to pack away his racing gear and look for gentler challenges. "The last time I saddled up was at Temuka in 1932. I won three races and called it a day forever."[18]

"He was a gentleman at every stage of the game, winning, losing or training for the next. You had to sign nothing with Phil. If he said that he'd be there, he was there. His word was as good as a stamped agreement."[16]

N.Z. Champion Cyclist

PHIL O'SHEA

Phil O'Shea on the track
– probably at English Park
Stadium in Christchurch.

Tinwald Cycling Club Collection

COACH OF CHAMPIONS

Phil O'Shea lived for cycling. He gave himself to it with more grit and determination than most of us can comprehend. But after the magnificent match races with Opperman in 1929 and 1930, his performance dived. Newspaper articles from November and December 1930 piece together O'Shea's fall from form. A bad crash at a race in Temuka in October left him with a dislocated shoulder that was slow to mend. Speculation was rife. Would the champion make the Christmas meet at Temuka – an event he hadn't missed in years?

Ultimately, O'Shea was forced to accept that he could not be ready in time and pulled out. Frustrated with this setback, he occupied his recovery time by helping young riders adjust their bikes and was soon observed instructing "15 riders in the art of pace-following".[1] He also formed the Jones Cycles Cricket Team, but after a few winning games he was hit in the eye by a cricket ball and forced onto the sidelines once more.

When his shoulder and eye had healed, O'Shea returned to racing, with mixed success, for one last season, before accepting the inevitable. In 1932, at the age of 42, he called it quits. Where does a champion cyclist go from there?

Aficionados who wanted to talk tactics would often find the champion sitting on an apple crate at the back of the shop, quietly building wheels.

From 1909 to the mid 1920s, O'Shea had been sponsored by Jack Suckling of Speedy Cycles and for much of that time had also worked for Suckling in his shop. In 1925, O'Shea switched to another Christchurch shop, Jones Cycles. He rode their bikes and worked there as a coach and mechanic – as well as taking on the role of shop figurehead. A life-size photo of the champion, set in a massive frame, held pride of place on the wall at the end of the counter.

This was a shop for serious racers. Aficionados who wanted to talk tactics would often find the champion sitting on an apple crate at the back of the shop, quietly building wheels. "It is always a pleasure to O'Shea to help young cyclists and would-be cyclists who ask his assistance in training, choice of a suitable cycle and other advice on the sport," claimed one newspaper report.[2] However, O'Shea never pushed himself or his sport on anyone.

Above Jones Cycles was a gym with weights and stationary training bikes. O'Shea had spent much time training in the gym and, when he finished road racing in 1923, he began coaching other road riders there as well. One of his first protégés was Harry Watson, who later gained fastest time in the Waimate to Christchurch race five years in a row, smashed the Taranaki Round-the-Mountain record and in 1928 was the first Kiwi to compete in the Tour de France.

Being coached by O'Shea was a privilege that gave a rider more than just sound training advice and excellent tactical strategies. Being coached by

"the master" also gave a psychological edge. After winning the 1928 Timaru to Christchurch, Bertram Arnst, like many O'Shea trainees, emphasised the value of O'Shea's efforts. "All credit is due to Phil O'Shea who coached me," he told the reporters, "and I have to thank him for my win."[3]

In 1932, when O'Shea retired from racing altogether, he expanded his coaching to take on track riders. Usually a rider would approach him – but not always. In the late 1930s, just after completing his second bike race, a young Ray Knight was walking away from the finish area when he noticed a familiar-

Harry Watson, the sole scratch rider, is about to start the Timaru to Christchurch Road Race. To the right of Watson is Phil O'Shea, next to the then Prime Minister, George Forbes. To the left stands Mrs Walter, the race organiser. Photo taken 1935.

Watson Collection

*"No smoking. No drinking.
And no going out with
naughty girls ..."*

looking man sitting on the footpath.

"Do you know who I am?" the man asked.

"Just," responded Knight. "I just know who you are. You're Mr O'Shea."

"That's right," O'Shea replied. "I train the good bike riders. What I'm looking for is a good boy. Just by what I've seen, you might foot the bill. ... Come in and see me at Jones' bike shop next week."

Ray was thrilled by the prospect and arrived at Jones Cycles on the Monday, eager to hear what O'Shea had to say. After telling Knight he showed promise, O'Shea offered to coach the teenager – with conditions. "If I train you, you've got a lot of things to give away to be a champion. Do you understand that?"

O'Shea's three main rules were clear: "No smoking. No drinking. And no going out with naughty girls. Now you go away and have a big think about that."

Ray did just that and returned a few days later to agree: "I'll give all those things away for a year and we'll see how we go, and if we're going good, we'll box on, and if we're not, I'll give it away."[4]

Knight didn't "give it away". Under O'Shea's tutelage, he quickly pedaled to the top of the amateur ranks, even beating the amateur champion Frank Gross in a 100-kilometre road race. When O'Shea advised him to switch to the cash ranks to earn money at the outbreak of World War Two, Knight leapt at the chance. Although he found this a tough move, it further improved his riding, and over the

Phil O'Shea served as a race
official for over 50 years.

O'Shea Collection

"He was the mastermind, there's no doubt about that."

next decade he won every New Zealand track title at least once.

In 1945, O'Shea successfully changed Knight's training schedule and helped him to victory in the classic Timaru to Christchurch Road Race.

O'Shea was renowned for his uncanny ability to assess the opposition – both their strengths and weaknesses – and for his intuitive sense of tactics. He would give Knight specific instructions on how to execute a particular race: when to hold back, whose wheel to sit on and at what point to jump – right down to the lamp post Knight should start sprinting from. Years later, Knight still attested, "It was all due to O'Shea. He was the mastermind, there's no doubt about that. He did all the thinking, and I did the riding. Without him, I might not have done nothing."[5]

Still looking for his own challenges, O'Shea took up the less punishing sport of golf. In 1940, he was reported to have won the Russley Cup, and later that year, with his wife, the Russley Cleek.[6] But he could never forsake cycling – he would ride his bike to work every day.

In January 1946, O'Shea opened Riccarton Cycles, a small shop in Christchurch. Here, he repaired bikes and sold Phil O'Shea bicycles. These were Austral Star bikes made by the Demurgh's bicycle factory in Christchurch, labelled with O'Shea Cycles transfers. In 1948, O'Shea received a much needed publicity boost when two of his bikes were ridden to victory in the Timaru to Christchurch Road Race. One, ridden by Cyril Arnst (nephew of Jack Arnst), was first across the line, and the other carried Graeme Milner to a junior record. As was the custom of the day, the winning bikes were placed in the sponsor's shop window with the riders' sashes or trophies.

O'Shea continued to coach many young riders, including champions such as Graeme Milner, Ken Jeffery, Gordon Kemp and Ken Giles. Milner recalled, "If O'Shea pushed your bike off [the start line], you were supposed to win."[7] Few of his protégés lived up to his expectations as well as Harry Watson. "Phil O'Shea was a tower of strength to me," Watson later declared, "not only in helping me keep fit but in keeping my cycle in tip-top order."[8]

In the 1950s, the New Zealand cycle industry virtually collapsed in the wake of an automobile boom. The last Christchurch bicycle factory, Cycleworths,

When Riccarton Cycles opened in 1946, petrol rationing and a lack of cars guaranteed a strong trade – but not for long.

O'Shea Collection

closed in 1956, and one of those made redundant, Stan Spence, bought Phil O'Shea's bike shop.

O'Shea was now in his 60s, but he continued working part-time for Spence until he was over 70 years old. He didn't always follow the retailers' motto of "the customer is always right". One Friday evening, a rider entered the shop at closing time, urgently needing several broken spokes replaced. O'Shea accepted the job and arranged for him to return for the wheel later that evening. When the rider picked up the wheel and started haggling over the repair bill, the old man saw red. With a pair of wire cutters, he slashed through the new spokes and suggested the customer find himself another bike shop.

AN OVERWHELMING RECEPTION

O'Shea was taken aback by the reception he received on his arrival in Australia.

In 1965, the 75-year-old O'Shea was invited to the jubilee of the Warrnambool to Melbourne Road Race as the special guest of his old rival Hubert Opperman. This was his first trip to Australia since last winning the classic race in 1923. As a quiet, modest man, O'Shea was taken aback by the reception he received on his arrival in Australia on 7 October. Opperman was by now Australia's Minister of Immigration and met O'Shea with a government car at the bottom of the aeroplane steps. The two followed the Warrnambool to Melbourne race in the car and were treated like sporting royalty. "I met many of the riders I knew in the early 1920s and many later ones who I had only read about. They gave me an overwhelming reception,"[9] O'Shea reminisced.

In contrast to the quiet O'Shea, Opperman had become an outstanding communicator. He had kept his reputation as a sportsman in Australia and become a successful politician. He was later knighted.

In the late 1960s, O'Shea fully retired from the bicycle business but still couldn't shake himself from the sport. He continued as a race official until he

Even after retiring, O'Shea continued working part-time in cycle businesses until the 1960s.

O'Shea Collection

An advertisement from the 1946 Waimate to Christchurch race programme.

E. Jayet Collection

was over 80 years old and was a lifetime member of a number of cycling clubs. In 1973, at the age of 84, he opened the new clubrooms of the Tinwald Cycling Club. He continued attending cycling events and avidly followed cycling, rugby and cricket events on his transistor radio.

O'Shea's frugality was renowned. He never had a mortgage or insurance and would crank his old Ford car to start it rather than use up the battery. No doubt one of the attractions of cycling was that it was so cheap! But O'Shea did have a generous spirit. As one rider recalled, "Phil O'Shea tried to put back into the sport more than he got from it." [10] He not only volunteered a huge amount of time towards being a cycle official and coach but also happily built up bikes for friends and family. During the Depression, uncomfortably aware of his comparative wealth, O'Shea was known to give credit to anyone wanting to buy a bicycle.

In his 80s, developing cataracts on both eyes gradually made life more difficult for O'Shea. When visiting the doctor, he would walk past the eyesight chart and memorise the bottom line to ensure he kept his driver's licence each year. But he seldom drove, preferring his bicycle. Pam Jeffery, wife of champion 1960s racer Ken Jeffery, recalls O'Shea "riding his bike to races at an old age, saving his car from getting wet!" And saving petrol as well, no doubt. The main reason

Long after retirement, Phil O'Shea could be found on the start line of many great races, such as here, circa 1965.

Owen Duffy Collection

though, as stated by an 81-year-old O'Shea, was: "There's nothing like it for keeping a bloke in good shape. I ride a bike nearly every day."[11] However, after O'Shea's wife, Elizabeth, died in 1971, he did drive regularly once a week to take flowers to her grave.

Phil O'Shea keeps active in his later years.

The Weekly Press, 14 March 1956

As he approached the age of 90, O'Shea's riding skills deteriorated, and he began to have accidents. A lifetime of cycle racing had taught him how to fall with minimal damage, but this didn't stop his relatives worrying. After cycling to visit family, he would stubbornly refuse offers of a lift home in a car but was happy enough to walk back with one of his grandchildren or a grand nephew.

In the twilight of O'Shea's life, his grandson, Philip Glubb, would visit him almost every day. Glubb remembers his grandfather from this time as a proud man, still determined but suffering from aches and pains – the result, in part, of a punishing career.

"I'll keep riding as long as I am able to because if I didn't, I think my health would suffer!"[12] Phil stated in a newspaper interview in 1922, and he remained true to these prophetic words. He cycled until 1979, when his poor eyesight finally forced him off his bike. The following year, at the venerable age of 91, Phil O'Shea died of influenza.

A LONG RIDE

A heart that seemed as if it would go on for ever
suddenly stopped beating yesterday morning.
Larry Saunders, 7 July 1980[1]

O'Shea's parents, Patrick and Nora, emigrated
from County Cork in Ireland around 1887. Nora
Mulane had eloped with Patrick, a man "beneath
her station" and was subsequently disinherited. After
a trying four-month voyage, their ship berthed in
Lyttelton, and the couple crossed the Port Hills to
settle in Christchurch. There, Patrick O'Shea set up
a successful transportation business. Two years after
Phil was born, the family celebrated the birth of
another son, Bob, and another two years on, a third
son, Jim. Their fourth and final child was a girl,
Eillee, born in 1896. As Phil was to recall in later
newspaper interviews, "I had a good up bringing …
I was never allowed to wander about the streets or
anything like that."[2]

Although often ill as a child, Phil was encouraged to take up sport. By the time he moved to the
cycling scene at the age of 20, he had already made a
name for himself in cricket and rugby, and officials
lamented his loss. "If he had kept up his Rugby, he
would have been an All Black. Nothing surer. He
was centre three-quarter in a youths' side … and, as

a stocky, straight runner with instinctive knowledge of the game, I never saw his equal," recalled Mr F. J. Sinclair, a well-known rugby referee.[3] Instead he wore the silver fern on his cycling top and by the time war broke out in 1914 was regarded as New Zealand's greatest cyclist.

By the middle of World War One, Nora O'Shea had become terminally ill. It is unknown whether Phil, serving on the other side of the world, was even aware of his mother's illness, which may have been some form of cancer. With determination that became an O'Shea characteristic, Nora clung on stubbornly until Phil's return from France in 1919, when she gave a sigh of relief and said, "I can die now, my boy's home safe."[4]

After his wife's death, Patrick O'Shea tried to rebuild his life. In the late 1920s, he gave up the transportation business and headed south to buy a farm near Balclutha. Phil recalled that there were so many rabbits on the farm, the very hills appeared to be moving. Unfortunately, the shift south was soon followed by the Great Depression. Patrick was unable to meet his mortgage repayments in those hard times, his farm was sold from under him, and he was forced to return to Christchurch, where he took up a job as a caretaker at the Villa Maria Catholic School. He died in 1938.

Phil O'Shea and Elizabeth Graham married in 1916. They had only one child, Doreen, who in turn gave them two grandchildren, Philip and Juliana. Elizabeth was an astute businesswoman who ran a

Patrick O'Shea with grandchildren.

O'Shea Collection

fruit shop in Fendalton after World War Two. Phil, of course, did the deliveries by bicycle. None of Phil's siblings or descendants took to competitive cycling – imagine the expectations if they had! Nevertheless, one grand niece recalled Phil quietly welcoming her family when they returned to live in Christchurch: he presented her and her brother with bicycles he had

*By his very actions he
inspired many bike riders.*

built for them himself. "You're in Christchurch now. You've got to ride bicycles," he explained.

O'Shea had no expectations that any of his family would follow in his cycling tracks, nor did he press anyone to take up the sport, but by his very actions he inspired many bike riders. There were those he raced against, the champions he coached and the many he congratulated as a race official. Beyond these accomplished sportsmen was a larger group of riders he knew little of – cyclists who never won a race but were motivated by O'Shea's sporting accomplishments to get on their bikes and have a go.

As one journalist explained, "... above all Phil was a gentleman. Not only did he grace sport, but he enriched it by his very presence."[5] Such descriptors as "modest", "tough", "honest", "extraordinary", "reliable", "cunning" and "star" have consistently been linked to Phil O'Shea's name, raising him to the lofty heights of hero.

"He was a man of self discipline and had complete knowledge of himself, both physical and mental, and knew not to do anything above or below his capabilities. This applied both in training and racing," said friend Alex McFarlane in an obituary.

A non-smoker and non-drinker he would deny himself anything that might affect his fitness. He was early to bed every night and led a very quiet life, believed in a simple diet, regular habits and plenty of fresh air. He would chew his food completely, believing that if you can't chew it, don't swallow it."[6]

In the days and weeks that followed O'Shea's death, friends and family, as well as older cycling enthusiasts, took time to recount the inspirational feats of his sporting career. Of these, you have already read, but behind the extraordinary athlete lies the wonder of a humble man. In old age, Phil sometimes commented that he really didn't know how he had won all those races. "I still can't believe it sometimes,"[7] he would marvel. Perhaps the frailty of old age reminded him of his sickly youth and a time when being a cycle racer was an improbable, tantalising dream.

Behind the extraordinary athlete lies the wonder of a humble man.

Great legends don't die when their bodies give way. The deeds that made them famous are recounted over and over, by word of mouth, on the printed page and across countless computer screens. O'Shea's presence is still felt, not only by those who have seen him race but also by aspiring young riders following in his tyre tracks. In the words of accomplished Canterbury road cyclist Phil Taylor: "O'Shea was like a ghost to us young riders: never there but always present."[8]

KEY RACE RESULTS

Phil O'Shea competed in an estimated 1420 races over 23 years. He won fastest time in the majority of handicapped events and between the ages of 23 and 36 rarely lost a scratch race.

1909
- 2nd in Chertsey Labour Day Sports 3-mile handicap – his very first race
- 1st across the line in Great Timaru to Christchurch Road Race (180 kilometres)

1910
- 3rd fastest time in Goulburn to Sydney Road Race (204 kilometres)
- 5th fastest time in Warrnambool to Melbourne Road Race (265 kilometres)

1911
- Fastest time in all three Canterbury Road Series events (20-mile, 35-mile, 50-mile)
- Fastest time in Christchurch to Timaru Road Race – New Zealand Road Champion
- Fastest time in Warrnambool to Melbourne Road Race – Australasian Road Champion: 8 hours 18 minutes

1912
- 1st in 25-mile road race with a fastest time of 54 minutes (average speed 44.7 kilometres/hour)

- 1st in 25-mile road race with a fastest time of 54 minutes (average speed was 44.7 kilometres/hour)
- 6th in Sydney Six-day Cycle Marathon (15 yards behind the winner)

1913
- 1st in several major track races, from ½-mile to 3-mile
- Unofficial world record for 10 miles racing for a team in 100-Mile Dunlop Relay Test (average speed was 42.4 kilometres/hour)
- Fastest time in Taranaki Round-the-Mountain Road Race – North Island Road Champion
- 1st and fastest time in Timaru to Christchurch Road Race, setting a new record of 5 hours 14 minutes 58 seconds for 180 kilometres – New Zealand Road Champion

1914
- Fastest time in Timaru to Christchurch Road Race – New Zealand Road Champion

1915
- 1-mile New Zealand Track Champion and set a new national record time (2 minutes 15 seconds)
- 5-mile New Zealand Track Champion

1920
- ½-mile, 1-mile and 3-mile New Zealand Track Champion
- Fastest time in New Zealand Road Championship races of 40 and 70 miles

1921
- 1-mile New Zealand Track Champion
- Overall New Zealand Track Champion (most points)
- South Island Road Champion
- Fastest time in 70-mile New Zealand Road Championships
- Fastest time in Timaru to Christchurch Road Race

1922
- 1-mile and 2-mile New Zealand Track Champion
- Fastest time in Timaru to Christchurch Road Race – New Zealand Road Champion
- Fastest time in Warrnambool to Melbourne Road Race: 8 hours 59 minutes 8 seconds – Australasian Road Champion

1923
- 1-mile, 2-mile and 3-mile New Zealand Track Champion
- 10-mile Australasian Champion
- Fastest time in Timaru to Christchurch Road Race
- Fastest time in Warrnambool to Melbourne Road Race: 7 hours 51 minutes 41 seconds

1924
- 2-mile New Zealand Track Champion
- 3-mile and 5-mile Canterbury Track Champion

1925
- ½-mile, 1-mile and 3-mile New Zealand Track Champion

- 2-mile Australasian Track Champion
- New Zealand Track Cycling Champion (most points)
- Match races against United States Sprint Champion Willie Spencer and others

1926
- Match races against Australian Track Champion Harris Horder and others

1927
- Match races against ex-World Sprint Champion Bob Spears and others
- New Zealand 1-mile record of 2 minutes 1 second

1928
- 2-mile and 5-mile New Zealand Track Champion
- New Zealand Track Cycling Champion (most points)

1929
- ¼-mile New Zealand Track Champion
- Match races against legendary Australian cyclist Hubert Opperman

1930
- ¼-mile and 1-mile New Zealand Track Champion

1932
- Competed for the last time, winning three track races at Temuka

THE SUITCASE

The suitcase that contained
Phil O'Shea memorabilia.

A few weeks before this book was due to go
to press, the authors received an unexpected
call from Phil O'Shea's granddaughter, Juliana
Feaver. While cleaning out her parents' estate she
had discovered a small brown suitcase. The contents
were a biographer's goldmine. There were photos and
newspaper cuttings, posters and race programmes,
O'Shea's address book and miscellaneous items, such
as a bow tie, spectacles and a bicycle tube. Some items
from the suitcase have been scanned to compile this
last-minute appendix.

(1) O'Shea (the winner) crossing the line.

First photos of Phil O'Shea
taken at end of 1909 Timaru
to Christchurch Road Race.

A WILD STAMPEDE.

IN THE SIX DAYS' RACE.

SEVEN TEAMS DROP OUT.

SEVEN STILL LEVEL.

FRANCO-GERMAN TEAM LOSES LAPS.

There was a wild stampede yesterday morning in the six days' cycle race which is in progress at the Sydney Cricket Ground. With 18 teams in the race, the riders found the track uncomfortably crowded, and falls were occurring too frequently, with the result that several of the best teams in the race put their heads together, and went out to shake off the weaker combinations. The manner in which the riders then tore round the track, with M'Namara and Keefe mostly in the lead, was hair-raising, and greatly delighted the spectators. Keefe, the record-breaking Tasmanian, started the rush at 10.45 a.m., and, with M'Namara relieving frequently, the pace was a scorcher. The track was a mass of riders, as all the team mates had been awakened to relieve their dropped partners.

A newspaper piece written during the 1912 Sydney Six-day Cycle Marathon.

Phil's head swathed in bandages at the end of the 1911 Christchurch to Timaru Road Race.

The final day of the 1912 Six-day Cycle Marathon in Sydney.

O'Shea being bandaged minutes after finishing in Timaru, 1911.

O'Shea Collection

1913   1913   1913   1913

Fun at Geraldine, St. Patrick's Day

It was fast and furious. A lot of Cyclists had journeyed down to Geraldine, each with a mount, determined to show PHIL O'SHEA how to ride. They had large handicaps, Mr. O'Shea was on scratch, but the others forgot what bike he was riding until they heard him buzz past on his **FLYING SPEEDY.**

RESULT OF THE RACING—

PHIL O'SHEA 1st in the half-mile off scratch
"   1st   "   one-mile   "
"   1st   "   three-mile   "

A. BONIS, who also rode the easy-running Speedy secured
1st in the 2-mile ; 2nd in the one-mile ;
2nd in the three-mile.

JACK SUCKLING, Maker of SPEEDY CYCLES, and Agent for the Reliable ROVER MOTORS

'Phone 2574.   114 MANCHESTER STREET

NOTE.—Make up your mind at once and secure a 1913 Model Speedy

Riders climbing Mount Moriac

Photos from the 1923
Warrnambool to Melbourne
Race.

Crowd waiting for Finish at Melbourne Haymarket.

PHIL O'SHEA, THE WINNER AND CHAMPION, WITH HIS "SPEEDY" CYCLE, FITTED WITH BARNET GLASS TYRES.

Seventy-five per cent. of the riders were mounted on other makes of machines, fitted with other makes of tyres, yet Phil O'Shea beat the lot from scratch. First, Timaru to Christchurch, 1909; Fastest Time, Timaru to Christchurch, 1911; First, Timaru to Christchurch, 1913, from scratch; Fastest Time, Timaru to Christchurch—a record for the race, 3hrs 14min 58sec. No other rider or machine in New Zealand or Australia can show such a record. All on his "SPEEDY" CYCLE, built by JACK SUCKLING, 114, Manchester Street, Christchurch.

O'Shea poses with his Speedy bicycle at the end of the 1913 Timaru to Christchurch Road Race.

Hats off to O'Shea as he is carried shoulder high at the end of the Timaru to Christchurch Road Race, in 1913.

Phil O'Shea wins
fastest time in the 1923
Warrnambool to Melbourne
Road Race by less than a
second.

The silver fern that Phil
O'Shea wore with pride.

The last known photo of
Phil O'Shea, cycling on his
90th birthday.

ACKNOWLEDGEMENTS

It is surprising how many people are involved in producing one small book. Without the following people, this biography of Phil O'Shea may never have been written.

Philip Glubb and **Juliana Feaver (née Glubb)**, grandchildren of Phil O'Shea, shared their time and knowledge as well as access to a suitcase full of photos, newspaper clippings and other memorabilia.

The Whitireia Diploma in Publishing student team of **Jackie Bedford**, **Anna Craig**, **Celestina Sumby** and **Penelope Whitson**, guided by **Rachel Lawson**, helped publish this book.

Christchurch historian **Bernard Hempseed** wrote a large profile on O'Shea in 2004 and reviewed this manuscript.

Road cycling aficionado and freelance copywriter **Jim Robinson** helped knock the initial drafts down to size and liven it up.

Cycle historian, event organiser and keen competitor **Simon Kennett** reviewed the manuscript with a critical eye.

Ian and **Stella Arnst** reviewed the manuscript and supplied books of invaluable newspaper clippings and photos.

Ian Gray reviewed the manuscript and researched several areas of technical interest as well as co-writing the prologue.

Graeme Milner, who was coached by O'Shea and helped in his bike shop, provided first-hand information for this biography.

Cycling champion **Ray Knight** was coached by O'Shea and interviewed by Jonathan Kennett in 2004.

We would also like to acknowledge the help we received from *The Press* in publishing an article seeking information about O'Shea; Keith Guthrie for providing access to his cycling literature; Ray Henderson for scanning and photocopying relevant information; Joyce O'Shea for giving the time to be interviewed; Alex McFarlane for providing an interview; Dick Cheyne for his research of English Park Stadium and Jones Cycles; Pam Jeffery for writing to us of her memories of O'Shea; Ian Watson (son of Harry Watson) for providing information and photos; the New Zealand Defence Force for providing O'Shea's army records; Matt Comeskey for his proofreading skills; Fred Vernall and David Strachan who sent letters and photos; Jim Sunderland for writing with information about O'Shea's bike shop; and also David Spence, Lorraine and Des Pither, Jim Tait, Simon Johnson, Bill Birch, Ron McGann and staff at the Alexander Turnbull Library (ATL), Christchurch Central Library and Canterbury Museum.

NOTES

Prologue

1. Newspaper article 35/071 copied in Arnst, *Early Cycling Classics 1913: Road Book 3*. Christchurch: home publication.

Rise of a Champion

1. Philip Glubb (O'Shea's grandson), in discussion with the author, November 2004.
2. *Press*, 1 November 1909.
3. *Christchurch Star-Sun*, 6 April 1940.
4. *Ibid.*
5. *Press,* 1 November 1909.
6. Mr E. Cummins in newspaper article 35/079 copied in Arnst, *Early Cycling Classics*. Christchurch: home publication.
7. Newspaper article 35/079 copied in Arnst, *Early Cycling Classics*. Christchurch: home publication.
8. *Press*, 1 November 1909.
9. *Ibid.*
10. *Ibid.*
11. *Star,* 9 October 1971.
12. Newspaper article 35/051 copied in Arnst, *Early Road Cycling Classics*. Christchurch: home publication.
13. *Press*, 1 November 1909.
14. *NZ Sportsman*, February 1948.
15. *Press*, 8 September 1911.
16. *Lyttelton Times*, 8 September 1911.
17. Newspaper article 55A copied in Arnst, *Early Road Cycling Classics*. Christchurch: home publication.
18. Unidentified newspaper article from the O'Shea Collection.
19. Newspaper article 35/071 copied in Arnst, *Early Cycling Classics 1913: Road Book 3*. Christchurch: home publication.
20. Newspaper article 73A copied in Arnst, *Early Road Cycling Classics*. Christchurch: home publication.
21. Newspaper article 35/071 copied in Arnst, *Early Cycling Classics 1913: Road Book 3*. Christchurch: home publication.
22. *Ibid.*
23. Unidentified newspaper article, Larry Saunders, 7 July 1980.
24. *Press*, 27 October 1913.
25. Newspaper article 35/069a copied in Arnst, *Early Road*

Cycling Classics: Road Book 3. Christchurch: home publication.

26.   *Christchurch Sun*, "Long Trail from Timaru", 1 October 1926.

27.   *Star*, December 1951.

The Bloody Roads of War

1.   Malthus, C. 2002. *Armentières and the Somme.* Auckland: Reed Books, p. 59.

2.   *The Great War, 1914–1918: New Zealand Expeditionary Force: Roll of Honour.* Wellington: WAG Skinner, Government Printer, p. iii.

3.   Drew, H.T.B. (ed.). 1923. *The War Effort of New Zealand.* Auckland: Whitcombe and Tombs Limited.

4.   Stewart, H. 1921. *The New Zealand Division: 1916–1919: A popular history based on official records: Vol. II. France.* Auckland: Whitcombe and Tombs Limited, p. 16.

5.   Cassell. 1917. *New Zealanders at the Front.* In Julia Millen, 1997, *Salute to Service: A history of the Royal New Zealand Corps of Transport and its predecessors 1860–1996.* Wellington: Victoria University Press, p. 115.

6.   Millen, J. 1997. *Salute to Service: A history of the Royal New Zealand Corps of Transport and its predecessors 1860–1996.* Wellington: Victoria University Press, p. 110.

7.   Carbery, A.D. 1924. *The New Zealand Medical Services in the Great War 1914–1918.* Auckland: Whitcombe and Tombs Limited, p. 183.

8.   McKenzie, C. (ed.). 'Chronicles of the NZEF, NZ Contingent Association', *1916–1919.* In Millen, 1997, *Salute to Service.*

Back in the Saddle

1.   *Christchurch Star-Sun*, 6 April 1940.

2.   *Ibid.*

3.   Military service records for Philip O'Shea.

4.   *Christchurch Star-Sun*, 6 April 1940.

5.   Unidentified newspaper article.

6.   *Press*, 21 January 1956.

7.   *Christchurch Star-Sun*, 6 April 1940.

8.   Opperman, H. 1977. *Pedals, Politics and People.* Sydney: Haldane Publishing.

9.   *Ibid*, p. 46.

10.   Unidentified newspaper article, date unknown, from O'Shea collection.

11. *Weekly News*, 14 March 1956.
12. Newspaper article 59A copied in Arnst, *Early Road Cycling Classics:Road Book 3*. Christchurch: home publication.
13. *Christchurch Star-Sun*, 6 April 1940.
14. Unidentified newspaper article, "Phil O'Shea Returns", date unknown, from O'Shea collection.
15. *Press*, 8 January 1966.
16. Philip Glubb (O'Shea's grandson), in discussion with the author, November 2004.
17. *Press*, 10 November 1923.
18. *Christchurch Sun,* 1924.

Whirlwind on Wheels

1. *Christchurch Star-Sun,* 6 April 1940.
2. *Christchurch Sun*, January 1925.
3. *Press*, 9 March 1925.
4. *Christchurch Sun*, 9 March 1925.
5. *Press*, 9 March 1925.
6. Letter from L.E. 'Hippo' Smith. (Smith was a Wanganui track cyclist who raced against Spencer at Athletic Park after O'Shea crashed.)
7. *Ibid*.
8. *Christchurch Sun,* 15 January 1926.
9. Newspaper clipping, Press Association, 5 March 1926.
10. *Christchurch Sun*, 25 October 1926.
11. *Press*, 3 February 1927.
12. *Press*, 7 February 1927.
13. Chany, P. 1975. *La Fabuleuse Histoire du Cyclisme*. Paris: O.D.I.L.
14. *Press*, 12 December 1929.
15. *Ibid*.
16. Smith, Max. 1966, *Game as You Like,* Auckland: Whitcombe and Tombs.
17. *Weekly News*, 14 March 1956.
18. *Christchurch Star-Sun,* 6 April 1940.

Coach of Champions

1. *Christchurch Sun*, 28 November and 5 December 1930 respectively.
2. Unidentified newspaper article, date unknown, from O'Shea collection.
3. *Press*, 8 October 1928.
4. Ray Knight in discussion with the author, 23 November 2004.

5. *Ibid.*
6. *Christchurch Star-Sun*, 6 April 1940.
7. From an interview with Jonathan Kennett on 20 March 2005.
8. Magazine article, source unknown, circa 1948.
9. Unidentified article from O'Shea Collection.
10. McFarlane, Alex. *Southern Cyclist*, Dunedin, 1980. Obituary for O'Shea.
11. *Star*, 9 October 1971.
12. Unidentified newspaper article, circa 1923.

A Long Ride
1. Newspaper article by Larry Saunders, source unknown, 1980, from Kennett Brothers collection.
2. *Christchurch Sun,* 1925.
3. Newspaper article 35/079 copied in Arnst, *Early Cycling Classics: Road Book 3*. Christchurch: home publication.
4. Philip Glubb (O'Shea's grandson), in discussion with the author, November 2004.
5. *Christchurch Star-Sun,* 7 July 1980.
6. McFarlane, Alex. *Southern Cyclist*. Dunedin, 1980.
7. Newspaper article by Larry Saunders, source unknown, September 1965. From Ian Gray collection.
8. *Weekend Herald*, 8 January 2005.

ABOUT THE AUTHORS

JONATHAN KENNETT

Since 1993, Jonathan has worked with his brothers Paul and Simon in Wellington on a variety of cycling projects including race organising, mountain bike park development and freelance writing. He co-authored *RIDE: The story of cycling in New Zealand*, and the best-selling *Classic New Zealand Mountain Bike Rides*.

BRONWEN WALL

A keen cyclist and freelance editor, Bronwen developed an interest in cycling legends while co-publishing *RIDE* in 2004. In tandem with Jonathan, she initiated the *New Zealand Cycling Legends* series.

INDEX

"YOU MUST NOT QUIT!"

When O'Shea retired from road riding in 1923, several hopeful cyclists vied for his position as king of the road, but it was "the mile eater", Harry Watson, who most often won the road championship title of New Zealand. This tall, quiet rider was a protégé of O'Shea's. Although he wasn't much of a sprinter, he excelled at long distances and set several enduring race records.

The most colourful event of Watson's cycling career was the 1928 Tour de France. His performances in Australia the previous year easily won him a place in an Australasian team led by Hubert Opperman. They set sail for the Continent in high spirits, with blissfully little idea of the pain and suffering ahead. As it turned out, this expedition was not only the adventure of Harry Watson's life but the feat that set him apart from other Kiwi champions simply because he was the first to complete the world's hardest and most prestigious cycling event.

Almost as soon as Watson arrived in France, he and his three Australian comrades had a sobering rendezvous with reality. Their European teammates did not show up, making theirs the smallest team in the tour; their fixed wheel bikes were laughed at by fellow competitors and their French manager knew next to nothing about cycling. European newspapers predicted they wouldn't make stage six of the 5375-kilometre 22-stage course. Indeed none of them had any experience of the tortuous trials awaiting them, such as the cobbled streets, the mountain passes and the long stages that had them riding into the night. But even as the European riders were dropping like flies, the four from down under struggled on, becoming favourite underdogs of the tour. Every day the captain, Opperman, would remind them that their countries had sent them to France and they "must not quit!"

The second title in this series, New Zealand Cycling Legends, *featuring Harry Watson, will be published in mid-2006.*